The Prophetic Way of Life

Academy of Self Knowledge Course TWO

By

Shaykh Fadhlalla Haeri

Publisher: Zahra Publications

ISBN (Paperback): 978-1-919826-29-5

http://www.zahrapublications.pub

First Published in 2012 as an E-Book

Paperback Published in 2021

© Haeri Trust and Shaykh Fadhlalla Haeri

All rights reserved. Except for brief quotations in critical articles or reviews, no part of this book may be reproduced in any manner without prior written permission from Zahra Publications.

Copying and redistribution of this book is strictly prohibited.

Table of Contents

Book Description	i
About Shaykh Fadhlalla Haeri	v
Overview	1
CHARTING THE WAY – MAP NO. 1: One Creator – Countless Creations	**3**
Charting the Way: Map No. 1 – Contents	4
Learning Objectives	5
Overview	6
Charting the Way – Map No. 1: One Creator – Countless Creations	7
Foundations – Charting the Way – Map No. 1: One Creator – Countless Creations	20
Charting the Way – Map No. 1: Exercises to Deepen Learning	24
Charting the Way – Map No. 1: Multiple Choice Quiz	25
CHARTING THE WAY – MAP NO. 2: One Truth – Countless Realities	**27**
Charting the Way: Map No. 2 – Contents	28
Learning Objectives	29
Overview	30
Charting the Way – Map No. 2: One Truth – Countless Realities	31
Reflection 1	35
Reflection 2	37
Reflection 3	41
Foundations – Charting the Way – Map No. 2: One Creator – Countless Realities	43
Charting the Way – Map No. 2: Exercises to Deepen Learning	47
Charting the Way – Map No. 2: Multiple Choice Quiz	49
CHARTING THE WAY – MAP NO. 3: Patterns in Existence – Allah's Ways	**51**

Charting the Way: Map No. 3 – Contents   52

Learning Objectives   53

Overview   54

Charting the Way – Map No. 3: Patterns in Existence – Allah's Ways   55

Reflection 1   60

Reflection 2   62

Reflection 3   64

Foundations – Charting the Way – Map No. 3: Patterns in Existence – Allah's Ways   67

Charting the Way – Map No. 3: Exercises to Deepen Learning   70

Charting the Way – Map No. 3: Multiple Choice Quiz   71

CHARTING THE WAY – MAP NO. 4: Prophet Muhammad – The Role Model   73

Charting the Way: Map No. 4 – Contents   74

Learning Objectives   75

Overview   76

Charting the Way – Map No. 4: Prophet Muhammad – The Role Model   77

Reflection 1   82

Reflection 2   84

Reflection 3   85

Reflection 4   88

Foundations – Charting the Way – Map No. 4: Prophet Muhammad – The Role Model   91

Charting the Way – Map No. 4: Exercises to Deepen Learning   94

Charting the Way – Map No. 4: Multiple Choice Quiz   95

CHARTING THE WAY – MAP NO. 5: The Qur'anic Prescription for Life   97

Charting the Way: Map No. 5 – Contents   98

Learning Objectives   99

Overview   100

Charting the Way – Map No. 5: The Qur'anic Prescription for Life   101

Reflection 1	106
Reflection 2	108
Reflection 3	110
Reflection 4	111
Foundations – Charting the Way – Map No. 5: The Qur'anic Prescription for Life	113
Charting the Way – Map No. 5: Exercises to Deepen Learning	116
Charting the Way – Map No. 5: Multiple Choice Quiz	117
CHARTING THE WAY – MAP NO. 6: Acts of Worship	**119**
Charting the Way: Map No. 6 – Contents	120
Learning Objectives	121
Overview	122
Charting the Way – Map No. 6: Acts of Worship	123
Reflection 1	142
Reflection 2	144
Foundations – Charting the Way – Map No. 6: Acts of Worship	148
Charting the Way – Map No. 6: Exercises to Deepen Learning	151
Charting the Way – Map No. 6: Multiple Choice Quiz	153
CHARTING THE WAY – MAP NO. 7: Relationships and Transactions	**155**
Charting the Way: Map No. 7 – Contents	156
Learning Objectives	157
Overview	158
Charting the Way – Map No. 7: Relationships and Transactions	159
Reflection 1	165
Reflection 2	166
Foundations – Charting the Way – Map No. 7: Relationships and Transactions	169
Charting the Way – Map No. 7: Exercises to Deepen Learning	173
Charting the Way – Map No. 7: Multiple Choice Quiz	175

CHARTING THE WAY – MAP NO. 8: Towards Perfection & Enlightenment — 177

- Charting the Way: Map No. 8 – Contents — 178
- Learning Objectives — 179
- Overview — 180
- Charting the Way – Map No. 8: Towards Perfection & Enlightenment — 181
- Reflection 1 — 193
- Reflection 2 — 195
- Foundations – Charting the Way – Map No. 8: Towards Perfection & Enlightenment — 197
- Charting the Way – Map No. 8: Exercises to Deepen Learning — 203
- Charting the Way – Map No. 8: Multiple Choice Quiz — 205

CHARTING THE WAY – MAP NO. 9: Principles and Foundations of Islamic Thought — 207

- Charting the Way: Map No. 9 – Contents — 208
- Learning Objectives — 209
- Overview — 210
- Charting the Way – Map No. 9: Principles and Foundations of Islamic Thought — 212
- Reflection 1 — 219
- Foundations – Charting the Way – Map No. 9: Principles and Foundations of Islamic Thought — 222
- Charting the Way – Map No. 9: Exercises to Deepen Learning — 225
- Charting the Way – Map No. 9: Multiple Choice Quiz — 227

CHARTING THE WAY – MAP NO. 10: Culture and Civilization of Muslims — 229

- Charting the Way: Map No. 10 – Contents — 230
- Learning Objectives — 231
- Overview — 232
- Charting the Way – Map No. 10: Culture and Civilization of Muslims — 233
- Reflection 1 — 242
- Reflection 2 — 243

Foundations – Charting the Way – Map No. 10: Culture and Civilization of Muslims   245

    Charting the Way – Map No. 10: Exercises to Deepen Learning   248

    Charting the Way – Map No. 10: Multiple Choice Quiz   249

CHARTING THE WAY – MAP NO. 11: The Individual and Society   **251**

    Charting the Way: Map No. 11 – Contents   252

    Learning Objectives   253

    Overview   254

    Charting the Way – Map No. 11: The Individual and Society   255

    Reflection 1   264

    Foundations – Charting the Way – Map No. 11: The Individual and Society   265

    Charting the Way – Map No. 11: Exercises to Deepen Learning   268

    Charting the Way – Map No. 11: Multiple Choice Quiz   269

CHARTING THE WAY – MAP NO. 12: Remedies and Prescriptions for the Wayfarer   **271**

    Charting the Way: Map No. 12 – Contents   272

    Learning Objectives   273

    Overview   274

    Charting the Way – Map No. 12: Remedies and Prescriptions for the Wayfarer   276

    Reflection 1   290

    Reflection 2   292

    Final Note – Advice to the Seeker   295

    Charting the Way – Map No. 12: Exercises to Deepen Learning   297

    Charting the Way – Map No. 12: Multiple Choice Quiz   299

E-Books By Zahra Publications   **301**

    General E-Books on Islam   301

    The Qur'an & Its Teachings   301

    Sufism & Islamic Psychology and Philosophy   302

Practices & Teachings of Islam	*304*
Talks, Interviews & Courses	*305*
Poetry, Aphorisms & Inspirational	*306*
Autobiography	*307*
Health Sciences and Islamic History	*307*

Book Description

This volume of work corresponds to the entire Course TWO on the Prophetic revealed path that the Academy of Self Knowledge (ASK) has offered in the past.

We have renamed it to *"The Prophetic Way of Life"* and put together all 12 lessons (known as maps in this book) of the course into this single book for the convenience of the students who would go through the entire course, doing the exercises and quizzes at their own pace.

The course unveils the Prophetic path, enabling people who have studied the cosmic design to maintain inner reliability and reference points. This experiential journey offers keys to the awakening of the heart and its nourishment by means of its purification. Based on the cosmology/view that the heart is the connecting point between the soul (the eternal), and the self (the ephemeral), the course focuses on transformation through awareness and the practices of the Prophetic path. This way of transformation includes understanding accountability, and performing structural responsibilities while being continually aware of the soul and higher consciousness.

Having studied and gained an appreciation of the blueprint of life, students can now learn how religious practices are transformational tools to enlightened awakening. This course teaches the student how to navigate through the challenges of this world while constantly referring to the limitless zone of absolute perfection that produced and sustains this world. It illustrates to the seeker the fact that no one can stop striving for perfection, and yet no one can attain perfection for any durable time. This is because the One Source that contains all these perfections owns and possesses the entirety of creation, and not the other way around. God's perfect attributes permeate all of existence, which bind, unify and drive creation towards fulfillment. The objective of this course is to enable the seeker to love the One unconditionally, and deal with multiplicity rationally. The maps specifically deal with the following matters:

Charting the Way – Map No. ONE: One Creator – Countless Creations

This map explores how we may achieve our highest potential as created beings by conscious worship of our original Source.

Charting the Way – Map No. TWO: *One Truth – Countless Realities*

In this map we learn about how our relationships with each other and our inner cosmology represent changing realities against the backdrop of a singular and unchanging truth.

Charting the Way – Map No. THREE: Patterns in Existence – Allah's Ways

This map looks at how perfection underpins everything in existence, whether or not we perceive it as such, and how it is made possible for us to access guidance from Allah.

Charting the Way – Map No. FOUR: *The Prophetic Model of Muhammad*

Map Four teaches us that all prophets brought essentially the same divine message and that the Prophet Muhammad's greatest miracle for all mankind, for all time, is the Qur'an.

Charting the Way – Map No. FIVE: The Qur'anic Prescription for Life

In this map the role of the Qur'an as the mirror for all creation is discussed; a mirror in which individuals and society as a whole are reflected and which guides both to live according to precepts laid down in it.

Charting the Way – Map No. SIX: *Acts of Worship*

In Map Six we are shown the vital link between acts of worship and a heightening in our awareness of the divine.

Charting the Way – Map No. SEVEN: *Relationships and Transactions*

The power of correct intention and the importance of our relationship with our original source are discussed in this map.

Charting the Way – Map No. EIGHT: Towards Perfection and Enlightenment

Map Eight teaches us about the power of the present moment as it is only the moment that contains within it divine perfection and the seeker who grasps this is set on the right course to enlightenment.

Charting the Way – Map No. NINE: *Principles and Foundations of Islamic Thought*

This map analyzes the tremendously cohesive influence of Islam and the Prophet Muhammad's exemplary life on disparate communities and nations.

Charting the Way – Map No. TEN: Culture and Civilization of Muslims

A further analysis of the cultural aspects of Islam and how the authentic prophetic teachings and cultural influences have mingled to positive and ill effect is done in this map.

Charting the Way – Map No. ELEVEN: *Individual and Society*

This map looks at how our outer reality reflects our inner and vice versa, and the inseparable connection between individuals and the societies they create. It reiterates the binding force that faith and its rituals provide, which serves to unify the individual and society.

Charting the Way – Map No. TWELVE: Remedies and Prescriptions for the Wayfarer

Book Description

This map aims to provide an overview of the hierarchies of spiritual growth. An understanding of these hierarchies is important for anyone who wants to live in an enlightened way while adhering to the ideal code of conduct bequeathed to us by all prophets and especially the Prophet Muhammad.

About Shaykh Fadhlalla Haeri

Acknowledged as a master of self-knowledge and a spiritual philosopher, Shaykh Fadhlalla Haeri's role as a teacher grew naturally out of his own quest for self-fulfillment.

He travelled extensively on a spiritual quest which led to his eventual rediscovery of the pure and original Islamic heritage of his birth, and the discovery of the truth that reconciles the past with the present, the East with the West, the worldly with the spiritual – a link between the ancient wisdom teachings and our present time.

A descendant of five generations of well-known and revered spiritual leaders, Shaykh Fadhlalla Haeri has taught students throughout the world for over 40 years. A prolific author of more than forty books relating to the universal principles of Islam, the Qur'an, and its core purpose of enlightenment, he is a gifted exponent of how the self relates to the soul, humankind's link with the Divine, and how consciousness can be groomed to reflect our higher nature.

The unifying scope of his perspective emphasizes practical, actionable knowledge that leads to self-transformation, and provides a natural bridge between seemingly different Eastern and Western approaches to spirituality, as well as offering a common ground of higher knowledge for various religions, sects and secular outlooks.

Overview

All of the Prophets indicated the same truth: that there is an Absolute Reality that germinates existence. It is timeless, beyond time and space, and from it has come multi-layers of lights. These lights have interacted with other layers of creational aspects, or other consciousness, resulting in multi-layered creations. These include many heavenly seen and unseen, and many earthly layers. We as human beings have many levels of consciousness. We have physical consciousness, of our hands, of our mind, of our sight, of our senses. Also, we have consciousness of our heart, whether it is clear or full of anger and rancor. The way of Islam gives a mapping whereby we can save ourselves from ourselves; ourselves from others; and others from ourselves. At all times we can use that mapping as a reference point of correct action.

Now the way (*dīn*) has also many zones within it. Some aspects are very structured and ritualistic. There is a right time to face a certain direction and disappear into nothingness, which is our prostration (*sajda*). Then at certain times repeatedly throughout our life we abstain from food and drink, and so on. All of our rituals within the *dīn* have deep meanings, which bring about spiritual growth and transformation. There are many layers of these meanings, which we become more and more sensitive to as we go along. The revealed books to so many Prophets, culminating in the Qur'an, contain many horizons of insights. There are some specific injunctions of do's and don'ts: be generous; do not hoard; do not fear for your provision. It is *Shaytanic*, from the lower aspects of the self. Do not harbor animosity for others; do not backbite; walk lightly on this earth. There are a lot of high-quality prescriptions from the Qur'an.

Then there is another wave in it, which is to do with the history of mankind, individuals as well as societies. Where are they now? What did they do? What did they leave behind? What state are they in now? The Prophetic tradition is that you leave this world according to the state that you are in. You will be resurrected according to the state in which you have died. We all want bliss. We all want the eternal garden because the soul has been designed with the feeling of that state within it. So, the question is how? We cannot do two things in this world at the same time. The how therefore becomes easy. Avoid those aspects, which are going to lower our consciousness, and our awareness, and get us imprisoned by the ego. Care more and more, and practice aspects of our life to heighten our awareness, reduce selfishness, and make us ready to leave this world as well as to stay in it. If we have a very clear map, we know where we are going to end up anyway, so we want to project and place ourselves in that position right now.

Our *dīn* is a way life, a way of thinking, a way of eating, a way of worshipping, a way of transacting, and a way of relationships. Every aspect has the appropriate courtesy. To begin with, for a child it's a bit difficult because he does not immediately see the benefit that he shouldn't eat while he is walking; he shouldn't drink while he is running, and so on. But as he gets older, he finds that these practices are beneficial because he does not get indigestion. All of these virtues, which are a result of practicing the *dīn*, are of immediate direct benefit. We are living at a time when society cannot help the family and individual very much because of the smaller households, and all of the other demands of pleasures and frivolous distractions. Therefore, simply giving orders to young people to follow rituals will not work. But if they realize that they can excel in their studies and exams by perfecting their *sajda* (prostration), how to disappear and have no thought in it, they will certainly do their *salat* (prayers) more enjoyably, and more on time. They will not miss it. There are benefits of *salat* at every level. So, we need to live our *dīn*, and to absorb the benefits of every aspect of the Qur'an and Prophetic teaching. We must be the first beneficiaries, otherwise we will be preaching without partaking ourselves, and that is hypocrisy. That is what so many so-called religious communities suffer from. So, the second course introduces us to the *dīn*, the *shari'ah*, the way of life: the way of thinking, moving, transacting; what is correct, what is allowed and what is not; what is forbidden completely and what is despicable and to be avoided. It is all for our own sake. Allah does not need it. You and I need it in order to realize the light of Allah in our hearts. The course shows us how to transform vices into virtues, and how every aspect of the *shari'ah* is designed to bring about a shift and elevation in the level of our consciousness and awareness.

CHARTING THE WAY – MAP NO. 1:
One Creator – Countless Creations

This introductory map corresponds to Lesson ONE of ASK Course TWO and explores how we may achieve our highest potential as created beings by conscious worship of our original Source.

Charting the Way: Map No. 1 – Contents

- Learning Objectives
- Overview
- Charting the Way – Map No. 1: One Creator – Countless Creations
    * Consciousness
    * Returning to Source
    * Polarity
    * Self-Knowledge
    * Inner Cosmology
    * The Realms of Essence, Attributes and Action
    * Divine Presence
    * A World of Opposites
- Foundations – Charting the Way – Map No. 1: One Creator – Countless Creations
    * Qur'anic Revealed Knowledge – Allah 'The One Essence'
    * Relevant Prophetic Teachings – Allah 'The One Essence'
- Exercises / Multiple Choice Quiz

Learning Objectives

From this map, you will gain an understanding of:

1. Returning to the One Source (*Allah*) from which multiple realities emanate.
2. Ascending to the highest levels of consciousness and fulfilling our potential.
3. The nature of the Soul (*rūh*) and the spectrum of the Self (*nafs*).
4. What it means to be a conscientious seeker.
5. Complementary opposites and duality.

Overview

Every aspect of manifest existence is based on movement and change and yet what human beings tend to seek is stability and security. Solving this apparent enigma involves discovering the singular truth, the light of which is reflected in the soul and heart of all human beings. The human heart contains the one constant screen upon which ever-changing patterns and images flash and generate countless forms and ideas that originate from the One Source.

Charting the Way – Map No. 1: One Creator – Countless Creations

Higher consciousness is only realizable by withdrawal from lower consciousness.

Consciousness

Our purpose as aware human beings, is to make ourselves conscious of, or to 'realize', the One Essence. But we also know that this Essence is impossible to describe, perceive and therefore 'know' or comprehend in its totality. We may refer to it as pure consciousness, or God, or Allah, but these remain mere words and not a living and complete conscious realization. Over time, and by practicing deep meditation and reflection, we may begin to understand that there are ways to 'perceive' that are beyond the limits of our intellect and reasoning. This kind of perception is aligned with pure consciousness manifesting as infinite levels of conditioned human consciousness. It is beyond words and thoughts and feelings but still manifests in our more accessible consciousness and exerts a subtle but powerful influence over our lives and the lives of those around us.

Allah reveals that He is a hidden treasure and He loves to be known, thus He creates everything known or unknown to us. All admirable attributes emanate from the One Essence. Indeed, the fabric of life is inextricably woven from these attributes.

As a result, every human consciousness is driven to unify with this pure essence and to realize its own ultimate potential by it.

Returning to Source

All movement and change in the world is to do with ascending towards the highest possible consciousness. What we call evolution is also a progression towards the subtlest and the highest. All the multiple varieties of creation have emanated from, are sustained by, and are yearning to be united with the One Essence that permeates all within and beyond time.

While the soul dwells in the heart of the human being it remains pure potential energy. The struggle to achieve unity with the One Essence, which is a struggle worthy of the highest description and honor, begins when this potential energy is galvanized and unleashed through conscious, willing and proactive aspiration. It takes a focused and sustained conscientious effort to achieve the quantum leaps in consciousness that characterize the journey towards discovery of, and awakening to, the One. Being proactive in our aspiration is of far greater value than being an unaware, compelled, passive and inert creature.

The divine creator, the One Essence of all creation, is not subject to time or space or prone to the impact of any changes we experience in our earthly realm. He is the cause and the power behind all creation; He is the motivator and the witness of everything and therefore if we are conscious of Him to the extent that He permits us to be, then we embody the means by which He causes, motivates and witnesses in creation. He becomes the eye with which we see, the ears with which we hear and the hand with which we grasp (*Hadith Qudsi*, Sacred Tradition).

Creation follows a certain prescribed path or decree towards its final destiny, which is the One Essence, the origin towards which it was journeying all the time. This is the meaning of "from Allah by Allah to Allah". Every material thing, animate or inanimate, is subject to natural laws and limitations within time and space. Although humans have emerged from and are returning to the zone beyond, they ideally need to be constantly aware of this final return and hence live responsibly in the here and now. The conscientious seeker lives and acts responsibly with patience and understanding but also experiences the delights of deeper perception and insight that come from beyond the rationality and reason born of conditioned consciousness.

Polarity

Anything experienced in the realm of existence is balanced in a polarity of opposites: health / illness, love / hate, light / darkness. Anything that manifests in the world of consciousness must be perceived in terms of the spectrum of these opposites. Things may be totally dark or slightly or pure light. Human consciousness scans a horizon of experiences perceiving life as very desirable or very undesirable, joyful or miserable, with many variations in between.

We are programmed by the One Essence to experience these layers of shifting and conditioned consciousness. But the constant yearning and call from the One Essence is also in our hearts urging us on to our highest potential consciousness. This is what is meant by 'Allah calls us to Himself'. The inherent drive towards such a higher aspect leads some of us to turn away from the transient and ever-changing world. This turning away is not a renunciation of the world – because the prophetic path insists on a full engagement with life in all its aspects – but is a subtle spiritual avoidance of things that will stop us evolving towards higher consciousness.

Those who respond to the call remember at a profound level the passion for that eternal bliss and cannot settle only for the changing world of good and bad, desirable and undesirable. No one will ever be content in such a world because of its inherently uncertain nature. That is why we are enjoined to be "in this world but not of it", even though we are in a constant and full engagement with the world. By our very turning ourselves towards that zone of bliss beyond this world we become more self-accountable, constantly watchful and incredibly humble so we do not fall short of our own high aspirations. We chastise ourselves if we do anything that may prevent access to that zone.

Exercise One

"... from Allah, by Allah, to Allah"
Meditate on this truth for a few minutes. How does it relate to your own life as a seeker?

Exercise Two

"Higher consciousness is only realizable by withdrawal from lower consciousness"

Reflect on the statement and ways in which you as a seeker can 'withdraw from lower consciousness', at the same time living 'responsibly in the here and now'.

Self-Knowledge

When we reflect on the highest divine attributes (aspects of which are contained within our soul and heart – referred to as *rūh*) we find sameness and a 'gathered' quality within all human beings. This sense of being gathered is the foundation of harmony. But when we analyze the ego-self (also often referred to as the *nafs* or lower self) we become aware of differences, the foundation of most conflicts within ourselves and between ourselves and others. The lack of unity and alignment between the soul and the self *within* the individual is one of the primary reasons for these conflicts.

The soul is always in harmony with itself and others. It is like a ray of light that emanates from a source of light – it is not the source but essentially the same as the source. Or we can say that the soul is like a spark that emanates from a flame – where the spark is not the flame but essentially the same as it. In a similar way, diverse shapes and individuations emerge once embers collect around the spark, just like the human identity or personality. These individual differences are superficial, incidental and accidental while the light within the spark remains vivid as ever and owes itself to its source.

The Prophet Muhammad taught that *"The souls are divine agents. Those who know each other are in harmony, those who do not know are in conflict"*. The meaning of this tradition is that before the *rūh* enters the body it has knowledge of all the other spirits (*arwah*)[1] because they all emanate from the same source[2]. But once it comes into the body it is covered by the *nafs*, implying that it is in fact the *nufus*[3] that are in conflict and not the *arwah*. This is as it should be: life began from a totally gathered state and manifests in dispersion and diversity.

Self-knowledge will enable us to see the unifying source that underlies diverse and apparent opposite manifestations. This is returning to the point made earlier about seeing with a 'deeper perception' beyond the limited intellect. To understand our individuality, we need to uncover the unifying essence within ourselves, which will enable us to see it (Essence) reflected in all creation. Man is a miniature image of the cosmos and his own complex cosmology, briefly outlined below, is designed to allow this unveiling process to take place in a conscious way.

By means of knowledge of the self we can identify the lower tendencies of the self and, through that understand the higher attributes of Allah. This kind of knowledge requires us to try and comprehend a thing by its opposite. By being aware of one's meanness, one can visualize Allah's generosity, for instance. Transcending the *nafs* before death brings about wisdom and

---

[1] Plural of *rūh*
[2] Surah *al-A'raf* 7:172
[3] or *anfus* – plural of *nafs*

illumination. Fear of death is a clear indication that transcendence has not yet been achieved.

Inner Cosmology

Here are some key terms to which we will refer during this course:

The self (*nafs*) resembles a hologram that can reflect and reproduce ever-changing states and attributes. Its range covers the lowest qualities to the highest divine attributes. The *nafs* can act in the meanest as well as in the most generous of ways: fearful or courageous, impulsive or patient, silly or wise, agitated or peaceful, ignorant or illuminated.

The mind (`*aql*) is the faculty of rationality and reasoning. It is the foundation for civilized society, culture and tradition. The limitations of the mind are also the source of its power as a universal utility and how it makes human inter-relationships possible. Mind is vital to begin with until the illuminated heart supersedes it.

When the heart has been illumined, it penetrates all layers of the lower *nafs* and recognizes it and is vigilant over it. This is what is understood from the prophetic tradition that *"He who knows his Self knows his Lord"*. Access to your Lord is through your soul, which dwells in your heart.

The soul (*rūh*) is the divine ray which energizes and gives life to the self and its physical body. It is the ultimate and constant reference point for the *nafs*. The actions and experiences of the *nafs* are only possible to understand because of the *rūh*. During sleep dreaming occurs when the *nafs* is distracted or less dominant. Death occurs when both the *nafs* and the *rūh* depart and the body is returned to its earthly origin.

The heart (*qalb*) and its facets of monitoring, reflecting, witnessing and recording are the link between the *nafs* and the *rūh*. When the heart is clear of defects (hatred, suspicion, lust and so on), then it will reflect to the *nafs* the source of higher guidance – the *rūh* and divine light.

Good intentions and appropriate actions are needed to cleanse the heart, purify it and enable it to reflect the higher truth. Invocation (*dhikr*) and other acts of worship (*sawm, salat,* etc.) are also means of purifying the heart and increasing the remembrance of the Divine Being. Access to your Lord is through your soul, which dwells in your heart.

Exercise Three

Consider (A) someone you get on really well with and (B) someone you do not get on well within the light of the following:

Dispersion and separation, lower tendencies of the ego-self, the faculty of reasoning (*mufakkira* – see the book *"The Sufi Map of the Self"*), a pure heart and the *rūh* as a reference point for the *nafs*.

The Realms of Essence, Attributes and Action

As we noted above, life in our sensory world is based on movement, which means we live with and are influenced by constant change; hence we need to find a reliable and constant zone of reference that will assist us in dealing with and understanding the extent and quality of change. To illustrate this point, let us look at the concept of pain. I experience pain and a fever and that distresses me. I also know that I have experienced worse pain in the past. Within me, then, resides a reference to pain-free wellbeing as well as to a much higher degree of intolerable pain. Hence with adequate reflection on both I may find equilibrium in my current state.

The realm of attributes is subtler than that of the realm of action and manifestation. It is these attributes that provide the impetus for all action and physical existence. Even subtler is the essence of Allah which is hidden in His attributes. Witnessing and understanding the unity of actions and how it manifests comes first. Only then may we begin to comprehend the unity of attributes, all of which meet in the One Essence.

The universe is composed of infinite varieties of diverse and heterogeneous components: solids, liquids, gases, living, inanimate, seen and unseen energies, colors, galaxies, relative time and apparent infinite space. There is One unique power, however, that enables these existential realities to connect, relate and interact with each other: the Divine Essence; Allah, the Glorious, the ultimate unifier and source of all relative powers; the one unique, all pervading-Creator and Sustainer of time and space; the Light behind all lights and shadows.

What we all seek, consciously or otherwise, is the knowledge of this absolute truth. Allah's attributes – the Everlasting, the Merciful, the All-Knowing, the All-Powerful, the All-Hearing, the All Seeing, and so on – are the doors which lead to the divine. These attributes are what govern the universe. Access to this knowledge comes only through self-knowledge, negating the ego-self (another definition of which is the shadow of the light of the soul) whilst upholding the spirit and reading the true meaning and message behind experiences and events.

Divine Presence

The true purpose of life is to adore, glorify and worship Allah. Yet how can you be consistent in your commitment, love and submission to Allah unless you experience the Divine presence at all times? How can you be illuminated, awakened and enlightened if you are dominated or influenced by the ego-self? The evolved seeker acts upon what the heart transmits and by doing so is transformed and able to transform. Constant, faithful submission, humility and high expectations of Allah will open up channels of insight and spiritual drive leading to a reliable and steady inner awareness, which becomes the source of true joy.

The seeker believes and hopes; the awakened knows and relies on the eternal truth. The seeker looks for the light of Allah to guide. He benefits and progresses according to the actions of submission, humility, patience, generosity, letting go and so on. The awakened only sees the merits of these attributes as emanating from Allah and as decreed for the awakened to act accordingly.

It is recorded in a prophetic tradition: *"I take refuge in Your forgiveness from Your punishment / purification [unity of actions], and take refuge in Your mercy from your anger [unity of attributes], and I take refuge in You from You [unity of essence]. Oh Lord, do not let me rely upon myself, not even for a blink of an eye"*. This means that we are acknowledging that there is only 'You' at the source of all that appears, and within all that there is. 'You' are the outer and the inner, the apparent and the hidden.

Exercise Four

Make a list of four things which help you on this path. For each one grade at what stage you are on a scale of 1 – 10 (10 being the highest).

E.g., 10 minutes meditation a day (5)

A World of Opposites

It soon becomes clear to the sincere seeker that everything in creation is based on opposites. All physical creation or experience falls into, or is perhaps classified by, combinations of the following: 'outer' / 'inner', 'sensory'/ 'meaning', 'earthly' / 'heavenly'.

To illustrate this, let us imagine that I am standing before you presenting a discourse. It is an 'outer' event. You are looking at me and listening to me. It is also a 'sensory' experience for both of us. We are in the material / physical world and this event is therefore 'earthly'. So, we are undergoing an outer, sensory, earthly experience. Yet the purpose of my discourse is to share inner knowledge with you. So, the purpose and sharing has an 'inner meaning' and this makes it a 'heavenly' experience.

The two opposites are balanced. The root of every situation or event lies in its opposite. Ordinary physical or material actions can be given a higher purpose and direction by awareness of the related inner event. For example, eating a meal is an outer, sensory, earthly event.

However, if we eat with the intention to nourish our bodies in order that it may be used effectively by the soul and thus carry us on the journey to greater perception and enlightenment, we will see that the act can be placed in the categories of inner, meaning, and heavenly.

All events and experiences can be categorized according to any of eight combinations of opposites. These may be classified as:

Combinations of Opposites	*Example*
1. Outer – Sensory – Earthly	*building one's house*
2. Outer – Sensory – Heavenly	*building a place of worship*
3. Outer – Meaning – Earthly	*seeing someone in pain*
4. Outer – Meaning – Heavenly	*looking at someone praying*
5. Inner – Sensory – Earthly	*remembering a loved one*
6. Inner – Sensory – Heavenly	*reflecting upon the stars*
7. Inner – Meaning – Earthly	*heart overflowing with love for all creation*
8. Inner – Meaning – Heavenly	*meditating upon God*

These and other concepts will be discussed in more detail as we proceed with this course.

Exercise Five

How & why would you classify the following in terms of the categories given above?

1. Reading an ASK map
2. Playing a game with children
3. Enjoying a day out with your partner
4. Visiting a holy shrine

Foundations – Charting the Way – Map No. 1: One Creator – Countless Creations

- Qur'anic Revealed Knowledge – Allah 'The One Essence'

- Relevant Prophetic Teachings – Allah 'The One Essence'

Qur'anic Revealed Knowledge – Allah 'The One Essence'

Allah says:

> *"Say: He is Allah, Absolute Oneness, All, the Everlasting Sustainer of all. He has not given birth and was not born, and no one is comparable to Him."* (Surah al-Ikhlas 112:1-4)

Allah is the ultimate Divine Light, which is always present, representing the Absolute Essence from which all attributes, names and manifestations emanate. Allah's dominion encompasses whatever is known or unknown, and cannot be comprehended/encompassed or limited by creation's thoughts, concepts, indications or attempts. All creation strives towards Him and His qualities – the All-Merciful, All-Generous, All-Powerful, Ever-living, Beautiful One, the Perfect Light of Lights.

Allah's essence and original Light radiate and overflow into all realms of creation. Anything that exists, appears, or lives, has within it an aspect of this light, and thus it is in Allah's kingdom. We as descendants of Adam's tribe have within our innate nature (*fitrah*) a yearning and love for all the primal streams and shafts of lights, which have the beautiful and desirable qualities of Allah. These Attributes are referred to in the Qur'an and in the Prophetic teachings as the Most Beautiful or Glorious Names. Most of these Attributes are universally acknowledged by all faiths, communities and cultures as virtues or high qualities[4]. Indeed, sages, saints and great leaders often show a hint of some of these traits and qualities.

Allah says:

> *"He is the First and the Last, the Outward and the Inward; and He is the Knower of all things. It is He Who created the heavens and the earth in six days; then He established Himself upon the Throne. He knows all that enters the earth and all that emerges from it, and all that descends from the sky and all that ascends up into it. He is with you wherever you may be, and Allah sees all."* (Surah al-Hadid 57:3-4)

> *"Allah's are the most beautiful names, so invoke Him by them. Leave those who desecrate His names. They will be repaid for what they do."* (Surah al-A`raf 7:180)

The task for mankind is to relate and connect to the appropriate quality or Name and be engulfed and absorbed by its glorious quality to realize its immediate present reality. Each and every quality meets all of the other attributes in the all-encompassing One. This great mystery can never be

---

[4] Please refer to Map 8, *"The Sufi Map of the Self"*, under section: *"Divine Qualities & Attributes that the self yearns for"*.

resolved. It will dissolve and yield its truth when we ourselves submit and die into its truth. It is the death of the individual identity – the shedding of the accretions that a human being collects through life – that will reveal His supreme presence.

Allah's eternal presence and His glorious attributes have been there from before creation and will continue after the end of all creation. Our responsibility is to yield and submit to His signs through our needs, shortcomings and other dependencies. He has created us such that we submit, read the signs and follow with faith and confidence in His grace. All of His names, signs, attributes and qualities are signposts along His path. We are led by Him unto Him.

Relevant Prophetic Teachings – Allah 'The One Essence'

1. Truly Allah resembles no 'thing' and no 'thing' resembles Him; everything which enters one's imagination concerning Him is a misinterpretation.
2. "Praise belongs to Allah, Who cannot be perceived by touch or any investigation by means of the physical faculties. He cannot be understood by the five senses, and imagination cannot grasp Him. Anything sensed, felt or touched by the hand is created (and therefore not the Creator). Allah is Sublime, the Powerful; whatever is desired by Him comes into existence."

Charting the Way – Map No. 1: Exercises to Deepen Learning
(One Creator – Countless Creations)

Title:
What is the purpose of human existence? How might the seeker move towards fulfilling this purpose?

Word Length:
Between 500 and 1000 words.

Criteria:
You may find the following criteria useful in addressing the question:

1. A description of moving from lower to higher consciousness.
2. The nature of the soul and the self.
3. Dealing with duality.
4. Some references to your own experience.

Charting the Way – Map No. 1: Multiple Choice Quiz
(One Creator – Countless Creations)

*The purpose of this quiz is to test your own understanding of this map. Choose the **BEST** answer A, B, C, or D:*

Questions:

Q 1: Human beings will not reach their highest potential consciousness, unless they
    A. Evolve towards a higher form
    B. Reject undesirable experiences
    C. Turn away from the transient ever-changing world
    D. Retire completely from the outside world

Q 2: The main purpose of self-knowledge is
    A. To repent of the lowest qualities of the self
    B. To understand the true source of all attributes
    C. To avoid committing sins
    D. To appreciate one's own individuality

Q 3: The seeker becomes awakened when he/she
    A. Sees only Allah's hand in everything
    B. Follows the correct path of the believer
    C. Is always humble
    D. Forgets about the *nafs*

Q 4: Awareness of opposites is important because
    A. We can live a balanced life
    B. We can combine different types of opposites
    C. We can nourish our minds and bodies
    D. We can develop insights into inner meanings of events and experiences

Answers:
1: C.
2: B.
3: A.
4: D.

CHARTING THE WAY – MAP NO. 2: One Truth – Countless Realities

This map corresponds to Lesson TWO of ASK Course TWO. In this map we learn about how our relationships with each other and our inner cosmology represent changing realities against the backdrop of a singular and unchanging truth.

Charting the Way: Map No. 2 – Contents

- Learning Objectives
- Overview
- Charting the Way – Map No. 2: One Truth – Countless Realities
    * Seekers of Unity
    * The Right Code
    * Simple Living
    * Material World
    * Full Circle
- Reflection 1
- Reflection 2
- Reflection 3
- Foundations – Charting the Way – Map No. 2: One Creator – Countless Realities
    * Qur'anic Revealed Knowledge – Creation
    * Relevant Prophetic Teachings – Creation
- Exercises / Multiple Choice Quiz

Learning Objectives

From this map, you will gain an understanding of:

1. Divine Truth is absolute and is not subject to any changes or confined by time and space, nor can it be discussed, defined, or contained.
2. All that human beings perceive as 'reality' is relative and interactive and subject to change.
3. Conscientious seekers always refer to the Truth whilst acknowledging and engaging with changing realities.
4. Relationships between human beings need to be underpinned by a sound connection with the ever-present Creator, otherwise most human associations remain unfulfilled.
5. The perfect or universal man is he who does the right thing in the right way at the right time.

Overview

Absolute Truth is a quality of God and whatever is in the universe reflects to varying degrees the divine decrees, qualities, and timelessness that is divine but it does so in a relative way. We can conclude from this that Truth is eternal and every other reality reflects only an aspect of it.

Whatever occurs within the realms of time and space appears to be real for a period. There is no end to these 'realities'. The more durable an occurrence, the more it appears to be 'true'. Therefore, even the relative 'truth' we encounter here relates to sustainability and timelessness and always reminds us of the Absolute Truth…

Charting the Way – Map No. 2: One Truth – Countless Realities

The Absolute Truth is One, never changing, ever-present, beyond time and space and yet it is the cause of everything that is in time and space. There are numerous 'realities' within time and space. These realities change all the time within their varying life spans, but each reflects or encompasses within it an element of Truth. For example, it is real that one feels pain, yet it is also real that one loves peace. The pain in the foot is a 'reality' only for an hour, but love for peace is a reality forever. Both are real and complement each other and both reflect an aspect of the Absolute Truth.

Seekers of Unity

The unity underlying existence has been revealed through many different messengers. Many seekers of unity have assigned different names to their discoveries over time but found the same Truth underpinning their discovery. Sometimes it appears as a religion or a culture. Conscientious seekers always refer to the Truth whilst acknowledging and engaging with changing realities. One exercises reason and rationality whilst being aware of the original Light and essence (or soul), which is beyond, as well as within, rationality. However, something more practicable is needed for us to navigate our way through the world and our life-transactions.

The Right Code

On an earthly level of existence, the entire rationale of ethics and morality has always been to discern the nature of cause and effect and that of the relative world. Equipped with this understanding and guidance we are able to see more clearly the subtle and veiled Cause at its nucleus. If respect for this world and worldly morality does not lead to respect and courtesy towards the Creator then we are left with a barren and unfulfilling code with which to live by.

From the very earliest of times, awakened and enlightened people, including the first prophets, had a clear priority with regards to ethics, morality and conduct, and in their time, they placed greater emphasis on understanding Absolute Truth in its abstract form rather than on learning about existential realities; about how the world works.

The later, or Abrahamic prophets, culminating in the Prophet Muhammad, presented to their people a comprehensive view and understanding of the ever-present, constant Truth and urged them ceaselessly to interact with this reality in the correct way. Their aim in this was to raise the people under their guidance to their highest potential–the perfect representatives of divine Mercy and Truth for the perfect or universal man is he who does the right thing in the right way at the right time. For there is no constant act of perfection in the changing world of time and space, there is only the appropriate action at a specific time and place.

Simple Living

Those who inherited and correctly applied these teachings from the early messengers and prophets understood the connection between energy and form, or the abstract and concrete, and the right way to interact with each. This was because life was very simple and uncomplicated then. There was a clear understanding of the right conduct towards one's fellow man and there was the correct way to respond to natural phenomena in order to live in harmony with nature. In that simple way of living, daily life was intimately influenced by natural phenomena such as the seasons and weather cycles. Thus, it was easy for people to relate to both the physical and the unseen: these aspects or subtleties were substantially interwoven into the daily fabric of their lives.

Material World

As human beings became more urban and civilized and lived within far more rigidly organized structures, most of their attention began to focus on cause and effect in the realm of physical duality, which resulted in a less sensitive awareness of the subtle cause of creation.

This dislocation from unity and oneness is particularly well-illustrated in the way modern medicine is structured. In contemporary society, for example, a sick person to whom a complex combination of medication has been prescribed may suffer unpleasant side effects and the illness may become more severe. The subtle cause of the illness, however, may have been an emotional need or crisis all along, like a lack of love and acknowledgement, or the need for a more fulfilling life. With our current over-emphasis on the senses and physicality, we tend to become de-sensitized to the subtler cause. We are now once again at a point in time when there is a move towards a holistic and subtle approach to healing once more. As a result, a new application of the moral codes discussed earlier needs to be put in place.

Full Circle

Every human being at all times is on the path of discovering the Absolute Truth. We all yearn for the perfections that are the divine attributes. These attributes are the manifestations of the Absolute Truth in our world. We love wealth; in truth it is Allah who has boundless wealth. We love power; in truth it is Allah who is the all-powerful. We love knowledge; in truth it is Allah who knows all. We love life to continue; in truth Allah has no beginning and no end. And the soul, which contains all of the divine perfections and glorious attributes, lives on forever.

Indeed, each human being is a soul that knows the Truth all the time but must filter it through the individual self and experience the world through the lens of this self, however dark or shattered it may be. Whatever you observe or experience is a reality and the longer it lasts, the closer it is to Truth. To illustrate the point, eternal peace can never be attained in this world. Yet, the longer I feel peace inwardly the closer I am to Truth.

As stated earlier, the Absolute Truth manifests through all of the divine attributes, which we adore. Appropriate action is that action which brings about balance, equilibrium, and stability. Any action that moves even slightly towards that state is appropriate in the context.

Exercise One – Conscientious Seekers

"Conscientious seekers always refer to the Truth whilst acknowledging and dealing with the changing realities."

Reflect on an experience where you were able to 'refer to the Truth' and another one where you failed to do so. How did this alter your perception and the way you dealt with the situation?

Exercise Two – Absolute Truth and Temporary Reality

As you live a day in your life, consider how your experiences of temporary reality relate to absolute Truth"

e.g., Someone's behavior annoyed you – temporary reality which could reflect the soul's search for Absolute justice and courtesy.

Reflection 1

Higher consciousness is only realizable by withdrawal from lower consciousness.

"The Truth is One, never changing, ever present, beyond time and space, and yet it is the cause of everything that is in time and space. There are numerous realities, all within time and space. These realities change constantly, within their varying life spans, but each reflects an aspect of truth."

Truth is absolute and is not subject to any changes, or the vagaries of time and space, nor is it discussable, definable, or containable. The Prophet taught that we should not discuss Allah, for we will go astray. But we should ponder and reflect on His attributes, qualities and the perfections of Allah.

All realities are glimpses of this Truth and the more durable they are, the closer they are to Truth. It is real that I am hungry, but that reality will change after eating. It is real that I seek happiness, that reality is everlasting. That reality is more subtle and the quest for happiness lasts longer and its ultimate fulfillment is everlasting, therefore it is closer to truth. But actually, the quest for happiness and hunger are reflections of the same truth only on different levels of density/subtlety.

All realities are relative and interactive, and relate to or repel each other. The paradox or enigma of human beings is that we contain within us the Eternal Truth, which is the soul, and at the same time experience ever-changing realties. What is referred to as God, or Allah, is the source and originator of all the souls that are at varying levels of realizing the original divine Creator.

Every soul totally reflects and is loyal to its Lord. The Absolute Truth contains all the perfections that we yearn for in this world, such as boundless generosity, power, knowledge and wisdom, and the ability to create or destroy. Allah's qualities embrace all these attributes which are known to the soul.

The self admires these and moves in small degrees towards them, or occasionally against them. When it moves towards them it is called 'obedience', when it moves against them it is called 'disobedience'. The human self has been given this limited license to look up to the soul and its qualities, or turn towards its shadow.

The Creator's generosity is absolute, His power absolute, His knowledge absolute, and the soul of Adam contains all of these patterns. Since the individuality or the personality of Adam has arisen, the only way to know absolute generosity has been to experience relative generosity or meanness. Thus, to know any of these attributes, which are boundless and perfect and absolute, we need to taste an aspect of these or their opposites. We live in the zone of the relative which is governed by the Absolute, and the stamp of the Absolute is evident in every instant, everywhere.

Each human being is a soul, modified by the self, and which reflects the Absolute, in order to experience the relative. All relationships are relative and changing, for the word 'relationship' has its roots in the word 'ratio'.

Reflection 2

Higher consciousness is only realizable by withdrawal from lower consciousness.

"Awakened and enlightened people from earlier times, including the earlier prophets, had a clear priority with regard to ethics, morality and conduct, and the emphasis was much more on truth than on existential realities. The Prophet taught that the purpose of all ethics and morality has always been to help the self to evolve in consciousness towards its original essence – so we are prepared to see more clearly the subtle and veiled cause behind all existence."

Enlightenment or awakening means access to the truth within. As we are occupied and involved with ever changing worldly experiences, we need to refer to the zone of stability and constancy within our soul to make the right decision and choose the best direction. The more the seeker manages to transcend specific consciousness and awareness and refers back to pure consciousness and divine awareness, the more they are inwardly calm, stable and content. This is the ultimate objective in this life, which has been lived fully by all the prophets, messengers, sages and other enlightened teachers.

All matters of ethics, morality, obedience, and correct actions are to do with prolonging the experience of perfection as the manifestations of divine qualities. We desire to be well, which is to a great extent dependent on our relationship with food and care for body/mind. Allah is the source of all wellness. Adhering to moral values or religious boundaries are attempts to increase the channels between the self and the soul, which flow through the heart, and thereby increase the possibility of attaining wellness in a holistic sense. The soul resides in the 'heart' and the heart is the seat of the higher intellect – *mutafakkira* – which is linked to insights and inspiration and a genuine reflection of the Truth. If you want to have constant access to the One Absolute and enjoy wellness and perfection, then you yourself must be constant and steady in the performance of correct and appropriate actions.

You therefore cannot cover yourself with lies or hypocrisy. The human desires to prolong the experience of perfection and this dynamic can only be performed adequately if whatever we do is appropriate at that instant.

The definition of appropriateness is to do the right thing in the right way at the right time. But what is right?

Perfection in that instant is right. If you are to be put in that same situation again, you will do the same thing. You will act generously, for example, towards someone you feel is less fortunate than you, irrespective of other people's views or opinions. It is the reference to Truth or to Absolute perfection.

Often the most appropriate action is not necessarily always the rational or logical but may seem irrational. For example, if someone has suffered a financial loss, worldly 'logic' dictates that the person stop giving to others or stop being charitable. But in the context of transactions based on the desire for durable and holistic wellbeing, the opposite would apply: to be more generous and charitable. In this way the person is accurately reflecting and acting upon divine Absolute Generosity.

A generous act is very specific and is appropriate to a particular moment. The same act may be mean or inappropriate at another moment. Presenting your mother with a box of chocolates that you know she will distribute or enjoy, is a kind act, but to give that box knowingly to an individual who has diabetes would be inappropriate and insensitive. To cut a finger is criminal, normally, but to amputate a finger destroyed by gangrene is divine mercy. It is appropriate.

No intelligent human can ever stop working towards perfection at all times. Nor will you ever be able to attain it for any length of time. Like everything else, here is relative 'perfection' and there is Absolute Perfection. Whatever relative perfection we attain will always be subject to an end, decay and entropy. As soon as you get it, the context changes for the realm of absolute perfection contains and controls all, and this divine messenger, the soul, beams its lights from your heart, perpetually. We tend to miss the light and its message. Success means to be controlled by Him, consciously.

Exercise Three – Doing the Right Thing at the Right Time (appropriateness)

Reflect on two decisions/actions you have taken.

1. What factors influenced you?
2. What was the outcome?
3. Do you believe you took the right/wrong action/decision and why?
4. 4. Are there times when there does not seem to be any correct action?

Reflection 3

Higher consciousness is only realizable by withdrawal from lower consciousness.

The perfect or universal man is he who does the right thing in the right way at the right time. For there is no constant act of perfection in the changing world of time and space, there is only the appropriate action at a specific time and place. Every human being at all times is on the path of discovering the truth.

The origin of man is the command of Allah – '*Be!*' The soul is a subtle force, the origin of which is in another realm and cannot be directly experienced or intellectually understood. The presence of such a force is indicated by what is the experienced reality.

A divine breeze causes the coagulation of the first cells, which then derive nourishment from the earth of the womb and move through the various stages of growth into a discernible form. Man was formed in such a way to enable him to reflect upon his true origin.

In Arabic the root word of *rūh* (soul) is the same as that of *rih* (wind, breeze) and *rahah* (comfort, ease). The search for comfort and ease is ingrained in man's nature. The subtle force that results in the creation of man is divine, sublime and indiscernible by our limited intellect. The power of the intellect is derived from the *rūh* so how can it directly comprehend the nature of its originator?

The nature of man as described in the divinely revealed book is to be a collector, a gatherer, who wants increase and goodness, wants to avoid badness and filter out anything that might cause disharmony. That disharmony might simply be in the mind or in desires, without having a physical reality to them. While desires can remain just desires, they can, like the desire to steal, result in a physical reality. Nevertheless, every human being wants equilibrium, peace and wellness.

The purpose of man's existence is very clear as it is recorded in the Qur'an: *"And I have not created the jinn and man except that they should worship Me"* (Surah al-Dhariyat 51:56). The real purpose of creation is to know the true meaning of worship; and the word in Arabic implies complete harmony, the absence of resistance or friction. The verbal root of this word in one form is *abbada*, to make smooth. Through worship, life becomes smooth and, therefore, will be completely connected, unified and gathered. The journey becomes only an experience rather than an end in itself; it becomes a means to an end, when it leads to the timeless zone.

Foundations – Charting the Way – Map No. 2: One Creator – Countless Realities

- Qur'anic Revealed Knowledge – Allah 'The One Essence" – Creation

- Relevant Prophetic Teachings – Allah 'The One Essence" – Creation

Qur'anic Revealed Knowledge – Allah 'The One Essence' – Creation

Creation is rooted in the mysterious. It includes the worlds of the spirits, the angels, the jinn, and myriad aspects of the spiritual and material realms. Allah describes those of us who accept this as true as *"the ones who believe in the unseen"* (Surah *al-Baqarah* 2:3). While children live in their own little carefree world, they need to be told to groom themselves, to wash their hands and tidy their room in order to assume the responsibilities of adulthood. In much the same way, we too have to be constantly reminded of the vast, unfathomable, unseen worlds that are far greater than our seen world, in order to mature into perfection, the Creator has given us the potential for.

From the unseen world of *haqiqa*, or Reality, Allah reminds us: *"I was a Hidden Treasure and I love to be known, so I created."* The basis of creation is love. Its purpose is to know the foundation and essence of life, which is why we all love to know with absolute certitude. The mind will drive us on until we come to be sure. We are programmed to know.

Everything hinges on *tawhīd*, 'divine unity'. What we see as creation is a unified field that rests upon an unstructured, invisible foundation not subject to time and space as we know it. The soul of the human being emerges in the timeless zone, lives through the physical world (the inter-space), and moves back into the timeless zone towards the Absolute. We realize that we are in the inter-space between what seems tangible and what is beyond. All systems of knowledge, all the true prophets and teachers, and all true religions acknowledge this; one aspect of us relates to existential realities on earth, which are to do with cause and effect, while another keeps us attuned to our origin before time.

Allah says:

> *"Behold! In the creation of the heavens and the earth, and the difference of night and day, and the ships which run upon the sea and that which is of use to men, and the water which Allah sends down from the sky, thereby reviving the earth after its death, and scattering about in it creatures of every kind, and the changing of the winds, and the clouds subservient between heaven and earth, in all of these are signs (of Allah's sovereignty) for people who understand."* (Surah *al-Baqarah* 2:164)

> *"And among His signs is that He created mates from yourselves, that you may find tranquility in them. And He has placed between you love and compassion. Surely in that are signs for people who reflect. And of His signs are the creation of the*

heavens and the earth and the diversity of your tongues and colors. Surely, there are signs in that for those who have knowledge." (Surah *al-Rum* 30:21-22)

"The seven heavens and the earth and those in them praise Him, and there is nothing that does not glorify Him with praise, but you do not understand their glorification. Truly, He is Forbearing, Forgiving." (Surah *Bani Isra'il* 17:44)

"Your creation and your raising (from the dead) are only as (the creation and the raising of) a single soul. Indeed, Allah is Hearer and Seer." (Surah *Luqman* 31:28)

"The All – Merciful (Who) taught the Qur'an He created man, and He taught him (clear) expression. The sun and the moon move with precision. The herbs and the trees bow down in prostration. And the sky He uplifted and He established the balanced universal laws, so that you would not exceed this balance. So, establish the balance with equity and do not fall short in the measure.

The earth He has laid out for all creatures, therein are fruit and palms having sheathed clusters, husked grain and fragrant herbs. Then which of the favors of your Lord will you deny? He created man of clay like earthenware, and He created Jinn from a flame of smokeless fire.

Then which of the favors of your Lord will you deny? Lord of the two Easts, and of the two Wests, then which of the favors of your Lord will you deny? He has made the two seas flow; their sides meet but between them is a barrier which they cannot exceed." (Surah *al-Rahman* 55:1-20)

Relevant Prophetic Teachings – Allah 'The One Essence' – Creation

1. "Reflect upon the bounties of Allah, not upon the essence of Allah, for you will never be able to measure the extent of His power."
2. "Allah does not allow anything to exist without a reason: thus, He made a reason for everything and He made an explanation for every reason; He gave knowledge for every explanation and He made a door for every knowledge. Those who know this know it; those who are ignorant of it are ignorant of it…"
3. "Thus, in creation is Truth itself, if you possess sight, and in the truth is creation itself, if you possess intellect. If you possess both sight and intellect, then you see nothing therein but one thing, albeit in different forms."

Charting the Way – Map No. 2: Exercises to Deepen Learning
(One Truth – Countless Realities)

Title:
Discuss the relationship between Absolute Truth and multiple realities in creation.

Word Length:
Between 500 and 1000 words.

Criteria:
You may find the following criteria useful in addressing the question:

1. Definitions of 'Absolute Truth' and 'multiple realities'.
2. The role of Divine Attributes, appropriate action and human relationships. Give an example for each.
3. An explanation of how an enlightened being might deal with changing realities.

Charting the Way – Map No. 2: Multiple Choice Quiz
(One Truth – Countless Realities)

*The purpose of this quiz is to test your own understanding of this map. Choose the **BEST** answer A, B, C, or D:*

Questions:

Q 1: Seeking happiness is described as 'closer to the truth' than being hungry because
    A. Hunger can be satisfied but we can never be happy
    B. Seeking happiness reflects our desire for the everlasting perfection of Allah
    C. You can be happy even when you are hungry
    D. A true believer is always happy

Q 2: We need to experience the relative
    A. To submit to Allah's will
    B. Because we have to be tried and tested
    C. In order to know the absolute
    D. Because we are physical beings

Q 3: Acting appropriately means
    A. Adhering to *Shari`ah*
    B. Striving to act in line with the Divine qualities at all times
    C. Avoiding excess
    D. Living a moral life

Q 4: Human beings are called a 'paradox' or 'enigma' because
    A. Their creation is a mystery
    B. They are both animal and human
    C. They are capable of good and evil
    D. They encompass both earthly and heavenly aspects

Answers:
1: B.
2: C.
3: B.
4: D.

CHARTING THE WAY – MAP NO. 3: Patterns in Existence – Allah's Ways

This map corresponds to Lesson THREE of ASK Course TWO and looks at how perfection underpins everything in existence, whether or not we perceive it as such, and how it is made possible for us to access guidance from Allah.

Charting the Way: Map No. 3 – Contents

- Learning Objectives
- Overview
- Charting the Way – Map No. 3: Patterns in Existence – Allah's Ways
    * Universal Laws
    * Divine Perfection
    * Obedience to the Soul
- Reflection 1
- Reflection 2
- Reflection 3
- Foundations – Charting the Way – Map No. 3: Patterns in Existence – Allah's Ways
    * Qur'anic Revealed Knowledge – Allah's Ways
    * Relevant Prophetic Teachings – Allah's Ways
- Exercises / Multiple Choice Quiz

Learning Objectives

From this map, you will gain an understanding of:

1. That existence and life are based upon webs that relate and connect.
2. That existence in the cosmos reflects divine perfection at numerous levels, some of which can be described.
3. That we experience great harmony and ease when our will coincides with the universal laws (or Allah's ways).
4. That the Creator has laid out these perfect maps for our own sake, so that we may read, internalize and follow them.
5. That the illumined person sees perfection behind and within what appears to be imperfect.

Overview

Existence contains countless pathways that are crisscrossed by causal turns and relationships. Every entity in existence is subject to movement and change and the human being always seeks the origin and root of these outer experiences in order to be secure and content–a deep need within mankind. The door to this security and contentment is the soul that resides within the heart and reflects the Creator's attributes.

Charting the Way – Map No. 3: Patterns in Existence – Allah's Ways

We all experience life and living. This experience is based on webs that relate and connect. There are multiple layers of cause and effect, some very subtle and therefore hard to fathom and others of a physical, material, chemical or electromagnetic nature that are easier to understand. We have countless examples of the latter in nature. The stars and planets, for example, move according to set patterns and trajectories, which can be plotted and calculated. Similarly, the electron spins around the nucleus according to fixed patterns. Human consciousness also follows certain patterns, although we are, in most cases, unaware of how these are arranged.

Indeed, existence in the cosmos reflects divine perfection at numerous levels apparent or otherwise. Even chaos has its perfect patterns, which is contrary to what simple human rationality or reasoning can understand. Thus, whatever is in existence echoes the perfection of the Creator. While these multi-dimensional cosmic channels, webs and designs are so intricately interwoven that the human mind or intellect cannot comprehend them all, the soul contains within it the blueprint of all these cosmic aspects. When we 'know' something it simply means that the channel of knowledge within the soul has been activated by the external experience. That is how we come to 'know'.

Exercise One – Patterns of Existence

Make a diagram (mind map or spider diagram) or list showing the multiplicity of connections in your life, seen and unseen, many of which you may be unaware of. You could use the following categories: Relationships, work, food, and environment. Reflect on how much 'control' you have or do not have over any of them.

Universal Laws

The universal laws (or Allah's ways) do not ever change. We experience great harmony and ease when our will coincides with these existing laws and when it does not, we are disappointed and may refer to the situation as 'unfortunate' or blame it on 'bad luck'. This 'disappointment' is simply due to us trying to establish a channel or movement contrary to what is already decreed. An individual's or society's destiny is inherently wholesome provided they follow the interactive maps that guide existence all the time.

All rational human beings seek contentment, harmony and stability, but do so often in the wrong way and without the requisite skills. As a specific body and mind caught in time and space our conditioned consciousness naturally seems to dominate. The more attuned we are to the soul and pure consciousness, however, the less we are bound by our conditioned consciousness and therefore more able and willing to follow Allah's laws and patterns that lead us to wholesomeness.

Divine Perfection

Nobody can ever maintain the right balance or connectivity unless their conditioned consciousness uses pure consciousness as a reference point. Therefore, as discussed in Map TWO, in order to maintain our state of well-being we need to care for what is immediate and apparent whilst relating to the absolute at the same time. That is the meaning of the prophetic tradition: *"Have mercy upon those on earth, and He who is in heaven will have mercy upon you"*. Care for what you can and be aware of the universal source of caring. These two aspects are never separate. The Creator has brought about these perfect maps for our own sake so that we may read them, internalize them and follow them.

Our conscious turning towards this way of being is very important. Will and desire are entirely based on our love for perfection, which is a many-faceted thing. These numerous facets of perfection and perfect qualities emanate from the One Essence who is the all-permeating Creator. Adam in the Garden has no bodily needs and is as such unconfined by time and space. But he does not know the meaning of self-sufficiency, eternity, contentment, bliss, because he is already in a state to which we, in our earthly state, may only aspire. He has no contrasting reference point. As a soul he is nourished and satisfied (hence the symbolic references to 'eating' in the Qur'an) and knows nothing of hunger and loss. Once Adam and Hawwa (Eve) experience separation and an acute awareness of conditioned consciousness along with bodily needs for the first time they 'fall' to the earthly realm of duality and are caught in time and space.

The first human 'fall' to earth happened so we could ascend to the heavens with knowledge of Allah's divine perfection. All creation aspires towards its highest potential within the limitations that each particular species has. For humans, as we know, this is achieved with varying degrees of success.

The microcosm continues to multiply and adores Allah's divine attributes of expansion, presence and eternal ongoing. All life forms adore, yearn for and strive towards the opposite qualities of the Creator, which are within their souls. For example, evolved or spiritually mature human beings consider it desirable to be generous, forgiving, helpful, patient, etc. All of these are Allah's attributes. The soul knows them all, and when the self yields to them it finds harmony in the heart and in its surroundings. But when it does not, the opposite (such as anger, meanness, and so on) manifests within and without.

Obedience to the Soul

This is why a parent feels such responsibility for helping a child to learn to be obedient, which in turn is intended to make the child conscious of the presence of the Divine within his or her soul. The parent's or teacher's role is to liberate the child/seeker from the darkness of the ego or the self, and to point out that even the darkness is part of the mercy of the Creator, through whose light the shadow was formed in the first place. The more the seeker sees the light and perfection within the soul, the more he sees only perfection around him. Thus, the illumined person sees perfection behind and within even what appears to be imperfect.

The purpose of existence is based on the mercy and the generosity of the One ever-present Creator who has brought existence about, sustains it, and brings together the degrees of recognizing the ways of Him. Human beings are distinct from the rest of creation in their ability to transcend cause and effect through the magnificent potential of the mind to receive illumination from beyond its own limited scope of rational reasoning.

As discussed above, every human being has within himself a representative of the Creator – called the soul – that contains all the desirable attributes, and which calls us to recognize its supremacy through the rise of the ego-self of the 'person'.

As a child grows, he identifies with roles and says 'I am a teacher' or this or that, but when you ask the illumined person about his/her ability to change all the time and what it is within her that does not change, he/she will reply that the soul never changes. Thus, all experiences in this life, even on a mundane day-to-day basis, are only images projected on the main screen, which is the soul.

Exercise Two – Universal Laws & Divine Perfection

"This 'disappointment' is simply due to us trying to establish a channel or flow or movement contrary to that which is already decreed."

1. Think of a 'disappointment' you have experienced. How would you relate it to this statement?
2. 'No condition is permanent' is a Universal Law. Reflect on anything in your life which you have thought of as 'permanent' and remind yourself that it is impermanent.

Reflection 1

Higher consciousness is only realizable by withdrawal from lower consciousness.

"We all experience life and living. This experience is based on webs that relate and connect. There are multiple layers of cause and effect, some very subtle and therefore hard to fathom and others of a physical, material, chemical or electromagnetic nature that are easier to understand."

A human being lives and travels along an expanding spectrum of multiple layers of consciousness. The infant is conscious mostly of food and other immediate aspects relating to its physical comfort. A person's consciousness expands with the accumulation of experiences stored in the memory.

There is a hierarchy in our attention towards and the selection of what we are conscious and this hierarchy holds true at all times no matter how mature or immature we are. The first step in this hierarchy is physical safety, security, well-being, and then mental stability and clarity, and then the fulfillment of social needs, of belonging, identity, status, acknowledgement, material security, etc.

The highest level of this inclining consciousness is pure consciousness, which is experienced occasionally as 'oblivion' or non-existence – as if our personality and all that we associate as our identity no longer predominate. There is a displacement of the 'location' of thoughts in that they are no longer dictated by 'self'-*ishness* but by the self in submission to the soul, and this obviously has a bearing on our actions. So, it is natural for human beings to seek such 'oblivion' and which is why misguided people seek oblivion through drugs, etc. They are looking for the same thing but in the wrong place and in the wrong way and seek to escape from the seemingly unending oscillation between cause and effect in their daily lives.

As stated earlier, one major difference between human beings and other types of creation is the human ability to rationally experience cause and effect and go beyond these. We deal with numerous events as they happen but also relentlessly yearn for the zone of absolute truth or constancy. This leads to the zone of pure consciousness, which other animals do not seem to be able to access. The most distinctive human quality is our ability to be conscious of our consciousness of consciousness. Thus, emotional and spiritual growth is directly linked to the extent of our self-reflection and self-awareness, until we realize that pure consciousness is in our core, beckoning us towards it all the time.

Simply put, we do not experience pure consciousness all the time because we are being affected by a specific consciousness – which we then label 'good' or 'bad'. You may be concerned about the welfare of your cousin or whether you have performed your prayers properly. All true religious practices train the seeker to always be at the edge of pure consciousness. *Salat*[5], for example, is a prelude to disappearing from this world in the *sajda*. Regular connection to that zone in which you transcend relationships and all realities, plugs you into the highest truth, which is the fountain/source of all realities, and you are thereby spiritually nourished.

---

[5] *Salat* is the act of formal prayer, and *sajda* is the prostration in the prayer.

Reflection 2

Higher consciousness is only realizable by withdrawal from lower consciousness.

"Indeed, existence in the cosmos reflects divine perfection at numerous levels apparent or otherwise. Even chaos has its perfect patterns, which is contrary to what simple human rationality or reasoning can understand. Thus, whatever is in existence echoes the perfection of the Creator."

The Creator is absolutely perfect and all His creation in every format reflects that perfection at all times. All of creation emanates from Allah, is sustained by Allah and returns to Allah, willingly or otherwise. Allah Himself is the Guide to Himself, for in truth, there is none other than Him. Therefore, all creation adores and desires Allah's attributes. The all-Generous, Powerful, Majestic, Everlasting - thus Allah's way is based on His light, power and knowledge.

In our attempts to emulate His perfections, such as power, wealth and dominance we tend to fail, because to humble us is a part of His generosity. Humility is the only attitude that allows us access to the Divine Presence. Allah's patterns of existence and the infinite varieties of His laws do not change; thus, we say His decrees or laws do not change. But destiny can change because it is the result of travelling along these channels. For example, in this life you are subject to multitudes of streams, some beautiful and calm, others like torrents. The streams crisscross the terrain and you are obviously affected by the stream you have dived into, possibly inadvertently - destiny is partly in your hands and partly not.

The turbulence we sometimes experience in life can be puzzling, especially if we think we have not done anything wrong. But if we consider calmly and rationally how chaos arose by looking at all the forces and factors that brought it about, we can see that it followed universal laws but their interaction was discordant, and so the outcome was as well. The friction of rocks below the earth's surface and the heat coupled with tectonic movement has naturally resulted in a volcanic eruption. Immense forces combined to produce this natural phenomenon; the human response then, quite naturally, is to avoid the volcano.

The ego-self is to be humbled while the soul is ever noble, and when the self synchronizes its will totally with the divine will, which is accessible to the heart, then the meaning of the verse: *"certainly the lovers of Allah have neither grief nor fear"* (Surah *Yunus* 10:62) becomes clear. In this case the seeker has synchronized his will with the cosmic divine will.

Thus, when we are in the midst of worldly struggles and we condemn a situation and consider it 'bad' or 'unfortunate', it is only for a specific, short-lived period that it seems inappropriate. But it is in fact completely apt. You consider it unlucky when you twist your ankle on a stone but both the stone and your foot have been performing their worship by moving according to the divine laws. The stone and the foot are in a state of worship but perhaps you are not!

Reflection 3

Higher consciousness is only realizable by withdrawal from lower consciousness.

"The descent to earth is only to ascend back to the heavens with the knowledge of Allah's divine perfection. All creation aspires towards its highest potential within the limitations that each particular species has."

Let us consider the divine attributes of *al Hayy* (The Ever Living), *al Qadir* (The Most Able), *al Muqit* (The Sustainer), as Sami (The All-Hearing), *al Basir* (The All-Seeing), *al Alim* (The All-Knowing), *al Muqtadir* (The All-Powerful). These seven great attributes are keys to our life experience in that they encompass most other qualities. We are programmed within the soul to love the virtues of generosity, kindness, tolerance, compassion, the ability to help others in sickness, or in need, or in giving them openings/opportunities in this life and guiding or nurturing them. We all love these attributes and can partake in them.

Some attributes we cannot partake in, for example, *al-Adhim* (The Magnificent), al Aziz (The All-Mighty), *al-Muhyi* (The Life-Giver), *al-Mumit* (The Bringer of Death) - they do not belong to us. In the case of a few attributes of Allah, we must take their opposite upon ourselves. For example, His glory - we must maintain our humility, and then His glory will be shown to us, not the other way around.

All life's experience is based on desiring and chasing after these perfect qualities. Sometimes Allah's will is such that the key to a virtue is actually a vice. He makes his beloved suffer a vice to properly turn him towards the virtue.

The attribute *al-Malik* is "the Possessor of the Kingdom," the Controller of all. Every entity in this existence is glorifying, worshipping, and adoring the attributes of Allah. But a man who thinks he possesses this characteristic of *al-Malik* without the accompanying humility and accountability can become a despot. Everyone wants to have the most powerful attributes of Allah because of their desire for Allah. Yet we already have Allah; we are already in the embrace of Allah; we are already the slaves of Allah. There is no escape from Reality; there is no escape from the laws of Allah.

Therefore, it is up to us to experience His laws, not in a dualistic or fragmentary fashion, but continuously and spontaneously until we see nothing but Allah manifesting through His different attributes. If an action seems to be incongruous, we need only reflect upon its cause to understand it. If the action is agreeable, then it has been done following His laws. If it is not, then inadvertently the action has been done incorrectly either because the actor/protagonist was in a hurry or he was in a state of *nifaq* (hypocrisy). If we were to think and hear correctly and systematically, everything around us would be coherent and systematic. That which appears to us to be incomprehensible, once examined, would reveal its inner meaning.

Every cause has an effect and every effect stems from a cause, except for the One and only Reality. This One that we speak of is *Ahadiyah*, 'Oneness,' not *wahid*, 'one.' It is not one of two; it is unique. Allah is His own Cause. Everything except Allah falls within laws that can be understood. All of creation is emanating from a root, from a cause that encompasses and controls it all without being tarnished, touched or affected by it. This is the puzzle into which we are born and which we are given our entire life to solve; a puzzle the solution of which is its dissolution. By dissolving ourselves, by abandoning ourselves and letting go of our hearts, not out of desperation and destitution, but through inspiration and perseverance, we may unify our actions and intentions fully to conform to the ways of Allah...

Exercise Three – Seeing Perfection in Every Situation

"Thus, when we are in worldly struggles and we condemn a situation and consider it inappropriate, it is only for a specific short-lived project that it appears inappropriate."

"Sometimes Allah's will is such that the key to a virtue is actually a vice. He makes his beloved suffer a vice to properly turn him towards the virtue."

1. Reflect on the meaning of Allah's 'Perfection' – in what way can situations we regard as bad be regarded as 'perfect'? E.g., wars and suffering.
2. Consider an occasion in your life where you suffered a vice which led you to virtue.

Foundations – Charting the Way – Map No. 3: Patterns in Existence – Allah's Ways

- Qur'anic Revealed Knowledge – Allah's Ways

- Relevant Prophetic Teachings – Allah's Ways

Qur'anic Revealed Knowledge – Allah's Ways

Allah says:

> *"Blessed is He who has the Kingdom in His hands, and He is able to do all things. He who has created death and life that He may try you, which of you is best in action. And He is the Almighty, All-Forgiving. Who has created seven heavens in layers? You cannot see any faults in the creation of the All - Merciful. Then look again, can you see any rifts? Look again repeatedly, your sight will return to you weakened and humbled."* (Surah *al-Mulk* 67:1-4)

> *"Alif Lam Mim. Do people imagine that they will be left to say 'We believe,' and they will not be tested with affliction'?"* (Surah *al-'Ankabut* 29:1-2)

> *"When harm touches man he calls on Us; then when We have granted him a benefit from Us, he says: 'This has come to me through my knowledge'. In fact, it is a trial, but most of them do not understand."* (Surah *al-Zumar* 39:49)

Relevant Prophetic Teachings – Allah's Ways

1. "If you were to trust in Allah with the trust which is due to Him, He would surely provide for you as He provides for the birds."
2. "Whoever has been given three things will not be denied three things; whoever has been given prayer, will be given the answer to his prayer, whoever has been given thanks, will be given increase, and whoever has been given trust in Allah, will be given sufficiency. Have you not read in the Book of Allah, "Whoever trusts in Allah, He is sufficient for him" (Surah al-Talaq 65:3), and "If you are grateful I would certainly give you more" (Surah Ibrahim 14:7), and "Call upon Me, I will answer you" (Surah al-Mu'min 40:60).
3. "Awaken your heart by reflection, and rise from your bed in worship at night, and trust in Allah as your Lord."

Charting the Way – Map No. 3: Exercises to Deepen Learning
(Patterns in Existence – Allah's Ways)

Title:
Discuss the meaning of 'Allah's Perfection' in relation to Universal Laws. How can human beings best live in harmony with these laws?

Word Length:
Between 500 and 1000 words.

Criteria:
You may find the following criteria useful in addressing the question:

1. A definition and examples of 'universal laws'.
2. Show how the meaning of 'Allah's Perfection' differs from our normal conception of 'perfection'.
3. An explanation of the attributes of Allah, higher consciousness, awareness, 'disappointments', and vices leading to virtues. You may give examples from your own or others' experience.

Charting the Way – Map No. 3: Multiple Choice Quiz
(Patterns in Existence – Allah's Ways)

*The purpose of the quiz is for you to test your own understanding of this map. Choose the **BEST** answer A, B, C, or D:*

Questions:

Q 1: Human beings can only achieve a certain degree of harmony if
   A. They pray regularly
   B. They align themselves with the Creator's will and decrees
   C. They understand that there is order within chaos
   D. They stop feeling disappointed

Q 2: The meaning of Allah's 'perfection' is
   A. That we cannot choose our destiny
   B. That we are imperfect
   C. That everything that happens is fully appropriate
   D. Not within our understanding

Q 3: The main difference between human beings and animals is
   A. Human beings can access pure consciousness through the process of rational thought
   B. Animals have no soul
   C. Humans are a superior creation
   D. Animals live in the moment

Q 4: The purpose of constriction and limitation is
   A. To make us realize we have no value
   B. To punish us for misdeeds
   C. To make us realize there is no heaven on earth
   D. To humble us and lead us back to our Creator

Answers:
   1: B.
   2: C.
   3: A.
   4: D.

CHARTING THE WAY – MAP NO. 4: Prophet Muhammad – The Role Model

This map corresponds to Lesson FOUR of ASK Course TWO and teaches us that all prophets brought essentially the same divine message and that the Prophet Muhammad's greatest miracle for all mankind, for all time, is the Qur'an.

Charting the Way: Map No. 4 – Contents

- Learning Objectives
- Overview
- Charting the Way – Map No. 4: Prophet Muhammad – The Role Model
    * The Message
    * Beings of Light
    * Role Models
    * Seeking Grace
    * The Miracle of Creation
- Reflection 1
- Reflection 2
- Reflection 3
- Reflection 4
- Foundations – Charting the Way – Map No. 4: Prophet Muhammad – The Role Model
    * Qur'anic Revealed Knowledge – The Role Model
    * Relevant Prophetic Teachings – The Role Model
- Exercises / Multiple Choice Quiz

Learning Objectives

From this map, you will gain an understanding of:

1. That Islam is a divinely revealed prophetic path that shows human beings how to submit to the absolute truth and live a noble life.
2. That the primary message of all the prophets was the same.
3. That the Prophet Muhammad made clear all that went before him and what was likely to be needed after him.
4. That the prophetic path of Islam reflects the original purpose of Adamic creation.
5. That the Prophet Muhammad's greatest miracle was the vast unveiling of the Qur'an.

Overview

Prophets are human beings who have harmonized their knowledge of the world with a profound consciousness of the unity underpinning this existence and beyond, away from the constrictions of time and space. A prophetic being is inwardly calm, certain and content while outwardly he is fully involved with other human beings with the intended goal of bringing about a deep realization of the Divine Presence in their lives at all times.

Charting the Way – Map No. 4: Prophet Muhammad – The Role Model

Islam is the prophetic path that enables human beings to realize the truth, submit to it, and thus live a noble life. Applied sincerely and with humility and awareness, that prophetic path of Islam leads us towards the realization of the ever-present Creator and Lord of the universe. Thousands of prophets and messengers have emerged from amongst numerous societies and cultures throughout the ages. The essence of the messages that all of them delivered was the same: firstly, that there is only One Creator and Sustainer of all the known and unknown realms of existence who has the exclusive right to be loved and worshiped, as to be known and worshiped is the purpose of His creating. Secondly, that for human beings, worshiping, knowing and loving Him entails self-denial and showing genuine compassion towards all creation.

Thus, all the enlightened prophetic beings and their followers submitted to this profound message and journeyed through many inner unveilings and outer struggles until they reached total certainty of the Omnipresent and Omniscient One.

The Message

The context, language and ways in which this message was conveyed differed considerably from messenger to messenger: human societies and cultures evolved in such a way that urbanization and civilization began to predominate and thus, from about the time of the Prophet Abraham, we find much similarity and consistency in the prophetic messages (as discussed in Map TWO).

The Prophet Muhammad clearly conveyed what went before him and what was likely to be needed after him. For this reason, he is accepted as the seal of the prophets. When you look back into the history of mankind, you will find that in most cases, *tawhīd*, or expounding the unity and oneness of the Creator, has been at the core of the teachings of all the religions.

However, with the passage of time and the influence of human failings coupled with the tendency to structure religion in ways that allowed it to be exploited by leaders or powerful members of a community, the original core and purpose of the message became adulterated and occasionally even drastically altered. The correct position is stated clearly in the Qur'an in the following and other passages:

> *Allah has said in His Book: Say (O Muslim): "We believe in Allah and that which is revealed to us, and that which was revealed to Abraham, Ishmael, Isaac, Jacob, and the tribes, and that which Moses and Jesus received; and that which the*

prophets revealed from their Lord. We do not differentiate between any of them, and to Him we have surrendered" – Surah *al-Baqarah* 2:136

Exercise One – The Core Message

"When you look back into the history of religions, you will find that in most cases, **tawhīd,** *or expounding the unity and oneness of the Creator has been at the core of their teachings."*

Talk to someone who follows a different path/religion from your own. Find out the core message of their path. Write down what unites you.

Beings of Light

The prophetic path of Islam reflects the original purpose of Adamic creation, with a soul that contains all the desirable attributes of Allah. Prophets and messengers have been societies' role models in terms of yielding to the Divine Presence and realizing the truth in their lives. Any description of these beings as 'perfect' simply implies that whenever they acted in this world of opposites, they had a spontaneous reference to the one constant truth to motivate their actions.

Therefore, strictly speaking, you could describe the actions of an enlightened being as appropriate for that moment as well as being the means by which perfection is manifest in that context. Allah alone is perfect at all times and all human beings desire to witness a flash of that perfection in the earthly realm they inhabit. An example of this is when you say you have succeeded, or your need has been satisfied for a moment, only to be faced with another set of challenges and needs that requires your attention.

Role Models

Prophets and messengers were role models in every aspect of their conduct and they were the masters of proper intention, action and behavior. The key to understanding prophetic perfection is that if you were with a prophet, you would not see anything other than perfection and you would know that he could not have acted in a different way at any given time.

The perfection of the unseen patterns inter-linking the absolute and the relative can become almost tangible through the prophetic way, where the unseen and the seen meet in perpetuity. The prophetic being is a heavenly entity with earthly shadows; and so are all human beings when they heighten their awareness of the Divine Presence.

All human beings have the potential of access to the divine light within their heart if the channels in the heart are not blocked by fear, anxiety, lust, hatred and other negative tendencies. Sincere seekers are like candles that can only be lit properly by kindling them with the prophetic light. The wick represents sincere dedication and commitment to the path and by yielding to the flame the pretensions of the self will be removed and the self will be illumined to its real nature, which is merely the shadow of the soul to which it aspires. Prophethood reminds us of the divine truth and all knowledge of the Creator – His attributes, His intentions and will, including the boundaries He has set for creation.

Seeking Grace

If the human self follows in these footsteps, then it is redeemed and tranquil, and if it does not, then by divine mercy and will, it will be subject to turmoil and anguish. Thus, everything we consider to be a test and trial are in fact divine gifts and warnings to return to the natural pattern. This corrective action is called *tawbah*. Often translated as 'repentance', it means two things: one related to the divine act (relenting or submission to it) and the other in relation to man's response to it (repentance). It originates as, and actually is, a divine act of grace and compassion–Allah's turning towards man–and is realized if man responds to it by doing penitence, which is another meaning of the word.

The Miracle of Creation

The Prophet Muhammad's miracle was the vast unveiling of the Qur'an, and the story of its revelation and subsequent dissemination is well known. But because of his acute and constant attunement to and synchronicity with the Divine will, whatever he said or did would gleam with a miraculous light and his close companions often described these acts as miracles.

All paranormal and psychokinetic activity is commonplace in the twilight zone between the seen and the unseen. Our human experience encompasses the hard, physical and material as well as the absolute subtle light permeating all existence. In fact, every instant in life contains miracle upon miracle but we are veiled from perceiving this because of excessive attention to our senses and physicality. There are millions of miraculous interactions in our human physiology yet we remain oblivious to them.

The way to enhance our awareness of these miracles is through knowledge and silent witnessing and watchfulness. If we understand the inner workings of the so-called hard, physical and material 'stuff' of life, then we are more finely tuned to the subtle Breath of the Merciful that enlivens us. Simply by turning our awareness towards the breath moving in and out of our lungs, the blood flowing in our veins, the way in which the seasons change or a spider builds its web, we become more aware of the miracles around us in every instant.

The higher the human being moves along subtle levels of consciousness, the wider and deeper are the vistas of what he 'sees' of the truth represented around him/her. He/she then also witnesses clearly the distortion and injustices perpetrated by un-evolved people.

That is why it is said that the closer one is to the ever-Present One the more we are afflicted by creational mischief. It is the price one pays for heightened awareness and insight; for there are no blessings in existence without their dark and, in reality insignificant, opposites. It is in this context that we may say that some prophets have been 'afflicted' during their mission on earth. Prophet Ayyub (Job) immediately comes to mind as does Prophet Nuh (Noah).

Reflection 1

Higher consciousness is only realizable by withdrawal from lower consciousness.

A prophetic being is inwardly calm, certain and content while outwardly fully involved with other human beings, with the intended goal of bringing about a realization of the divine Presence at all times.

Prophethood and Messengerhood

The prophet is a human being who is subject to all natural human experience and traits whilst connected to a unique reference point and source of guidance. He is the ultimate model of conduct for evolving human beings in that he acts in the right way and at the right time and in a way that is understood and approved by all people of intellect, wisdom and insight.

Prophethood transmits information regarding divine truths and realities which include knowledge of the Creator's Essence. All prophets and messengers have expressed direct knowledge of God. Some have also related messages to do with ethical boundaries, appropriate conduct and the natural laws.

The prophets' conduct and actions are always a model of the perfect human qualities- of generosity, understanding, sacrifice, justice, gentleness, courage and other virtuous traits befitting God's representatives on earth.

Their leadership and care for fellow humans encompasses the weak, the needy, the good and the wicked, and especially those serious in their quest for gnosis. The life of the prophetic being reflects what the proper path to the knowledge of God is, what is to be avoided and what is to be transcended.

CHARTING THE WAY – MAP NO. 4: Prophet Muhammad – The Role Model

All prophets and messengers have been endowed with miracles and other seemingly inexplicable powers and knowledge appropriate to their time and mission. The miracles of the Prophet Muhammad were the Qur'an and his noble way of living amongst one of the least civilized of human tribes. The way and life of the Prophet Muhammad, his conduct, practices and teachings are a living illustration of the Qur'an. The existential difficulties and afflictions that the Prophet Muhammad struggled through can be understood in the light of the revolutionary changes and new directions he brought to individuals and society.

The prophetic sacrifices in fulfilling the divine mission are negligible compared to the inner delights and divine intimacies with which they are graced. When the inner battle is won, the outer and physical struggles seem only a small price to pay.

Reflection 2

Higher consciousness is only realizable by withdrawal from lower consciousness.

"Islam is the prophetic path that enables human beings to realize the truth, submit to it, and thus live a noble life. This leads them higher and higher towards the realization of the ever-present Creator and Lord of the universe"

Muhammad, the culmination of the prophetic exemplar

At the time of the Prophet Muhammad human consciousness had reached a point at which the path of enlightenment could be described and followed without it being confined to a culture or race or geographical area. A few thousand years ago there were prophets in villages and some of the Judaic prophets were only acknowledged by a few households in a small area. Very rigid practices and habits were often part of the religion of some of these prophets, perfectly suitable for their immediate circumstances.

Generally, every successive prophet absorbed the meaning and the light of what had become evident before him. So, the knowledge revealed to the Prophet Muhammad encompassed the collective consciousness of all that had come before him. The way and life of the Prophet Muhammad, his conduct, practices and teachings are a living illustration of all such revealed knowledge.

In this context the Prophet Muhammad's way is the culmination of all knowledge, ethics and conduct and there is not much more to be added after him. The backdrop may be different, the civilizations may be less or more defined, but the inner maps remain eternal and all-encompassing.

Reflection 3

Higher consciousness is only realizable by withdrawal from lower consciousness.

"The Prophet Muhammad's miracle was the vast unveiling of the Qur'an. Because of his constant attunement to and synchronicity with the divine will, whatever he said or did would shine with gleams of miraculous light and the close companions often described his actions as miracles."

The Way of Muhammad

The natural development of the awakened self is to move from the discovery of the Divine Light within oneself – serving others with humility, selflessness and love – to the Creational Source that is behind all creational manifestation. After the retreat into the cave of awakening comes the return to society. After achieving control of the passions that constitute the lower self and having been illuminated one can only re-connect with creation, the highest manifestation of which is humankind.

The life of the Prophet and his experiences encompass a rich source of teaching for those who want to follow in the prophetic footsteps. He underwent practically every possible human experience as he fulfilled the roles of teacher, emigrant, merchant, head of the household, political and social leader, military commander, and judge and, throughout his life, the divine Seal of the Prophets. His nobility, humanity, magnanimity, courage, forgiveness, steadfastness, understanding and total devotion to Allah, the most glorious, were expressed in all these diverse situations common to the collective experience of mankind. His behavior and conduct became the ideal standard to be followed and from it the adjective *sunni* is derived.

Muhammad's way was the perfection of the prophetic way that began with the rise of consciousness in the Adamic model. The revealed Qur'an talks about all the prophets and messengers as having brought to their communities the one and only message of surrender into Allah, living a godly way in this physical existence before returning to another phase of being.

Muhammad is the culminating pinnacle of all the prophets and messengers. He embodies the completion of the collective prophetic consciousness that has come to mankind during the years of the final evolution and awakening of the higher consciousness within the human being. His message confirms all that went before and points out where distortion, misunderstanding and aberration have occurred. Thus, his message supersedes all those that came before it in a way that leaves no space for any doubt or misunderstanding, except for those who actively seek it and wish to create confusion for themselves and others, and those blinded by religious chauvinism.

Exercise Two – Prophetic Qualities

"The key to understanding prophetic perfection is that if you were with the prophet, you would not have seen anything other than perfection, and you would realize that he could not have acted differently."

Imagine you are with the Prophet. Why do you want to follow him?

Reflection 4

Higher consciousness is only realizable by withdrawal from lower consciousness.

"O Prophet, indeed We have sent you as a witness and a bringer of good tidings and a Warner, and one who invites to Allah, by His permission, and an illuminating lamp, and give good tidings to the believers that they will have from Allah great bounty." (Surah al-Ahzab 33:45-47)

The True Merits of Leadership

The soul in every individual calls the individual away from the constant illusions, delusions and distractions of the ego-self in order to establish itself as the reference point via a clear and pure heart. The soul is always there to assume its rightful internal leadership, and external leadership must correspond to and support it - otherwise it is not legitimate.

The leader of a community needs to reflect the same endeavor, which is to be content with what is necessary, have conviction and practice all the desirable virtues of human courage, loyalty, willingness to sacrifice, honesty and discipline, so that all actions are based on wisdom. From there on justice begins to take root. The ultimate justice is for everyone to recognize that they have never been independent of the One and only Source within; that is true divine justice that all human beings try to strive for on this earth with varying degrees of success and failure.

Good leadership brings about all the desirable human virtues, increasing and improving upon wisdom and justice, and this is what is meant by doing one's utmost to make leadership on this earth reflect the heavenly kingdom; to realize the *khilafah* (vice-regency) of man on earth according to divine intention (Surah *al-Baqarah* 2:30).

Although everyone knows this state is never attainable for any period of time, equally no intelligent person can ever stop trying to attain it. The prophetic model for leadership is the ultimate role model to be followed dynamically, not simply mimicked clumsily. If the Prophet Muhammad was concerned about discord among some of his friends we should reflect and imitate his concern but not necessarily in the specific way that he expressed it. When he wanted to visit a friend who was ill at a distance, he may have chosen to ride his best steed, whereas now you may drive your car. It is the visit to the patient that is important, not the means used to getting there.

The baby looks up to the mother as her provider and mirror and that is true babyhood. The healthy, secure, seven-year-old has a wider range of relationships but still has a sound reference point to rely on.

Therefore, conscientious parents do not want their children exposed to situations that may detract from their progress. The wise parents act as the guide for the child and lead it slowly and gently to the gate of the Lord in his heart.

Then the child understands that the wise parent was doing his utmost to place him under the Lord's instruction. But the child may only function in this world via the level of his consciousness at that moment.

As one grows towards maturity the inner mirror simply takes on the images that fall upon it and internalizes them, for it has no appropriate mirror with which to contextualize them.

For this reason, human beings need exemplary reference points in a worldly sense, which leads them to the ultimate reference point of the divine domain, which in turn encompasses both this world and the next. Therefore, for a serious seeker it is essential to find a mirror that is more perfect than his or hers to get the inner refined and the heart purified. The best such mirror is one that is closest to the prophetic example. It is important for the sincere seeker to have access to an awakened teacher as a guide and reference point in this journey.

Exercise Three – Leadership

As a follow up to the previous exercise,

1. Reflect on the qualities of a good leader.
2. Do you know any good leaders? How does their leadership differ from prophetic leadership?

Foundations – Charting the Way – Map No. 4: Prophet Muhammad – The Role Model

- Qur'anic Revealed Knowledge – The Role Model

- Relevant Prophetic Teachings – The Role Model

Qur'anic Revealed Knowledge – The Role Model

Allah says:

> "Mankind was one community, and Allah sent the Prophets to bring good news and give warnings. With them He sent down the Book with the truth that it might decide between mankind wherein they differed. Those to whom the Book was given differed concerning it, after clear proofs had come to them, through envy of each other. Allah, by His permission guided those with faith to the truth of that which they differed. Allah guides whom He wills to a Straight path." (Surah *al-Baqarah* 2:213)

> "We never sent a messenger except with the language of his people, that he might make (the message) clear for them. Then Allah misleads whom He wills and guides whom He wills. He is the Mighty, the Wise." (Surah *Ibrahim* 14:4)

> "Muhammad is the Messenger of Allah. Those who are with him strongly oppose those who cover up reality, and they are merciful amongst themselves. You see them bowing and prostrating, seeking grace from Allah. Their mark is in their faces from the traces of prostration. This is their description in the Torah. Their likeness in the Gospel is like sown corn that sends forth its shoot then strengthens it so that it thickens and grows up straight on its stalk, delighting the sowers that He may enrage the unbelievers with them. Allah has promised those among them who have faith and perform good actions, forgiveness and immense reward." (Surah *al-Fath* 48:29)

CHARTING THE WAY – MAP NO. 4: Prophet Muhammad – The Role Model

Relevant Prophetic Teachings – The Role Model

1. "He (Allah) desired to distinguish Himself by His Oneness when He veiled Himself in His light, and ascended in His sublimity and hid Himself from His creation, and sent Messengers to them that they may be the evident proof of Himself for His creation and that His Messengers to them be witnesses over them…"
2. "Allah has chosen prophets from amongst Adam's descendants who, through revelation, accept (divine) contracts and are entrusted with delivery of the divine message," and "He has sent His messengers amongst them and has sent His prophets one after another to fulfill the contract of the *fitrah* (the original, innate nature of man), and to remind them of the blessing which had been forgotten. Delivery of the message and calling men to Him is proof (of Him); the prophets transmit treasures of wisdom and knowledge and they show man the decreed signs."
3. "He has refused to accept the worship of anyone except those who obey and revere the messengers; and knowledge and love of the messengers is with Allah as is their dignity, honor and veneration."

Charting the Way – Map No. 4: Exercises to Deepen Learning
(Prophet Muhammad – The Role Model)

Title:
What are the core values which the Prophet Muhammad and other prophets taught? Describe the prophetic qualities. How can ordinary leadership be guided by prophetic leadership?

Word Length:
Between 500 and 1000 words.

Criteria:
You may use the following criteria as guidelines:

1. Explain two main core values taught by the prophets.
2. Describe four prophetic qualities with examples.
3. Explain four ways in which leaders can be guided by the prophetic way with examples. ('Leaders' include any kind of person in authority such as parents and teachers.).

Charting the Way – Map No. 4: Multiple Choice Quiz
(Prophet Muhammad – The Role Model)

*The purpose of the quiz is for you to test your own understanding of this map. Choose the **BEST** answer A, B, C, or D:*

Questions:

Q 1: Prophetic 'perfection' means that
   A. All Prophets are absolutely perfect
   B. Prophets are the best leaders
   C. Prophets are pure
   D. Prophets always act appropriately

Q 2: The reason we go through turmoil is
   A. God is punishing us for our misdeeds
   B. God has given Satan permission to annoy us
   C. God is warning us to return to correct action and thoughts
   D. Unbelievers are attacking us

Q 3: Muhammad is the culmination of Prophethood because
   A. No previous Prophet knew as much as he did
   B. He encompassed all previous revealed knowledge
   C. He was closer to God than any other Prophet
   D. He lived a much better life than any other Prophet

Q 4: The main purpose of good leadership is
   A. To protect people from enemies
   B. To ensure that laws are enforced
   C. To act like a parent to the people
   D. To reflect Divine Justice as closely as possible

Q 5: For most seekers a teacher is essential because
   A. A proper teacher acts as a mirror and reference for the seeker
   B. Seekers don't have sufficient knowledge
   C. Without a teacher a seeker might go astray
   D. Seekers are not virtuous enough to guide themselves

Answers:
1: D.
2: C.
3: A.
4: D.
5: A.

CHARTING THE WAY – MAP NO. 5: The Qur'anic Prescription for Life

This map corresponds to Lesson FIVE of ASK Course TWO. In this map the role of the Qur'an as the mirror for all creation is discussed; a mirror in which individuals and society as a whole are reflected and which guides both to live according to precepts laid down in it.

Charting the Way: Map No. 5 – Contents

- Learning Objectives
- Overview
- Charting the Way – Map No. 5: The Qur'anic Prescription for Life
    * Perfect Patterns
- Reflection 1
- Reflection 2
- Reflection 3
- Reflection 4
- Foundations – Charting the Way – Map No. 5: The Qur'anic Prescription for Life
    * Qur'anic Revealed Knowledge – Qur'anic Prescription for Life
    * Relevant Prophetic Teachings – Qur'anic Prescription for Life
- Exercises / Multiple Choice Quiz

Learning Objectives

From this map, you will gain an understanding of:

1. Divinely revealed knowledge relates to the inner dimension within us which makes us reflect Allah's ways.
2. The Qur'an is the transcendent word of the Transcendent Lord, Creator and Sustainer of all things.
3. The Qur'an itself is revealed knowledge and a light that illumines the patterns, meanings and purpose of existence.
4. The Qur'an contains the blueprint for the best manner of transacting with ourselves, our society and our Creator.
5. The Qur'an describes how each individual as well as the societies they live in will come to reap what they have sown in this world and the next.

Overview

Divinely revealed books encompass the whole spectrum of the metaphysical and physical worlds. In the Qur'an we find the unifying field in which multiple levels of unseen energies interact with things that are clearly visible to us. For the human being to discover his cosmology fully the self needs to evolve according to the divinely revealed prescriptions stated in the Qur'an.

Charting the Way – Map No. 5: The Qur'anic Prescription for Life

Every human being contains two dimensions of consciousness. One is perceptible, can be discussed using language and relates to the senses, the mind and the emotions. The other dimension of consciousness is to do with a pure consciousness or the soul, and forms our innermost core. Our life's journey demands maturity, a conscious move towards spiritual evolvement and the establishing of a sound connection between these two dimensions.

Divinely revealed knowledge relates to this inner dimension and its capacity to receive and reflect Allah's ways. The Qur'an, which speaks so eloquently about the Creator's patterns and designs within creation, was transmitted through a prophetic being well-prepared for the task in hand–to bring to a tribal people mired in ignorance the clear truth of Reality. But above and beyond this, the Qur'an has the ever-present Creator speaking, through angels or other means, to the prophetic being for mankind's benefit and for all time. The multi-dimensionality of this truth is vitally relevant to all conscious creation so it may orient itself towards its Creator.

The Qur'an is the transcendent word of the Transcendent Lord, Creator and Sustainer of all things. According to it, the process of creation began when Allah took the covenant from the soul of man with the question: *"Am I not your Lord?"* (Surah al-A'raf 7:172) From that point on every soul was exposed to all of the Divine attributes and qualities and transmitted them to each individual self. Once the self is prepared and fully attuned to the soul, exposure to the map of the Qur'an triggers its transformation.

This is why the Qur'an benefits everyone at different levels of their journey towards the Divine. The Qur'an may at first be rejected by the crude, egotistic self if the self is caught up in its own assumption and presumption of independence and separation from the all-Powerful Creator. It begins to yield and submit to the truth of the Qur'an, however, as it matures and when the heart begins to reflect the Qur'anic truth at all levels. That is the prophetic transmission, which can only be received with a purified heart; it cannot be touched except by those who are engaging in purification (*see* Reflections *section below*).

Throughout the history of humankind divine revelations have come to prophets. Several of these prophets are known to have received a divine book and are mentioned by name in the Qur'an. The final message that encompasses all that went before in these revelations is to be found in the Qur'an.

The root of the word 'Qur'an' is derived from the Arabic noun, which originally means 'collections'; *qara'a*, the verbal root, means 'to read' or 'to recite'. This divine book contains Allah's commands and the numerous facets of all created realities. His Oneness threads through everything known and unknown. *"Will they not think about the Qur'an? If it had been from other than Allah, they would have found much inconsistency in it."* (Surah al-Nisa 4:82).

The Qur'an is the foundation of the *din,* the life transaction, containing as it does Allah's ways, patterns, purpose and direction of creation. Through His Book, Allah reveals to us His unique Oneness and His Attributes. All aspects of the knowledge of the unity underlying creation, prophethood, the return to Allah (the Oneness), resurrection, heaven and hell, personal and social directives and commands and prohibitions – all originate from the Qur'an.

The Qur'an contains the blueprint for the best manner of transaction with oneself, society and the Creator. It is Divine Essence manifested in a transformative way, awakening the self to the everlasting Source within the heart.

Perfect Patterns

Allah's creation, its purpose and direction, is laid out according to perfect designs and patterns. In order for our innate nature (*fitrah*) to develop in recognizing and adhering to those inherently harmonious ways, we need to grasp the full code of the *din*.

The Qur'an unveils the way to Allah by Allah's mercy (*rahmah*) and equally identifies the cul-de-sac that draws us into confusion and destruction. It describes in detail the character, conduct and path of the believer and also the bleak picture of the non-believer. It highlights the pitfalls of the ego-self (*nafs*) and how one may sublimate and transform into an enlightened being.

Exercise One

If you are accustomed to reading the Qur'an, do both 1. and 2. If you are not familiar with the Qur'an do just 2.

1. Reflect on your relationship with the Qur'an – Which five divine attributes mentioned in the Qur'an have most relevance in your life?
2. What do you understand by 'divinely revealed'? What might the difference be between such a book and an ordinary work of advice and guidance?

As well as addressing the individual, the Qur'an also addresses mankind on a social level. This can be seen in the many references that enjoin right action and social justice, as well as the clear warnings about nations being destroyed by their own wrongdoing.

The Qur'an describes how each individual, as well as entire nations, will come to reap what they have sown in this world. Pure actions, prophetically guided, with spontaneous awareness of the Divine Presence, will result in illumination in this world in preparation for the Hereafter. Allah reminds us repeatedly in the Qur'an that the believer's responsibility is to perfect his or her worship through sacrifice, submission, inner contentment and constant striving. These are the keys to transformation for which every intelligent human being strives.

Exercise Two

"Allah reminds us repeatedly in the Qur'an that the believer's responsibility is to perfect his or her worship by sacrifice, submission, inner contentment and constant striving. These are the ingredients of transformation for which every intelligent human being strives."

Reflect on your self-knowledge. How would you rate yourself on the qualities mentioned above? (e.g., Am I in a state of inner contentment most of the time?)

Reflection 1

Higher consciousness is only realizable by withdrawal from lower consciousness.

"*Divinely revealed knowledge relates to this inner dimension and its capacity to receive and reflect Allah's ways. The Qur'an, which speaks so eloquently about the Creator's patterns and designs within creation, was transmitted through a prophetic being well-prepared for the task in hand-to bring to a tribal people mired in ignorance the clear truth of Reality. But above and beyond this, the Qur'an has the ever-present Creator speaking, through angels or other means, to the prophetic being for mankind's benefit and for all time. The multi-dimensionality of this truth is vitally relevant to all conscious creation so it may orient itself towards its Creator.*"

The Qur'an affirms:

"*Indeed, it is a noble Qur'an, in a Register well-protected, none touch it except the purified, [it is] a revelation from the Lord of the worlds.*" (Surah al-Waqi`ah 56:77-80)

The Qur'an here speaks of a mutual transaction between the Book and the one who takes guidance from it. Only he who purifies his intentions, words and acts, that is, he who purifies the entire transaction with his Creator, his fellow creatures and himself, is able to 'touch' or absorb the teachings from the pure and holy word of Allah (which is one of the meanings of the word, '*massa*' used in the quote above). This kind of interaction with the Qur'an will raise a person to increasing degrees of purity.

The Qur'an was first revealed to the Prophet Muhammad on the Night of Decree or Determination when he was 40 years old, but was fully unveiled gradually over the following 23 years of his life.

The specific occasions for the revelation of many of the verses have been narrated and recorded by the Prophet Muhammad's companions and progeny. The chapters revealed in Mecca generally address human beings and major aspects of the acts of creation, whereas most of the chapters revealed in Medina relate to the divinely revealed code of personal and social conduct, worship and other social and legal matters.

During the Prophet's lifetime the Qur'an was collected by several of his close companions. It was, however, during the Caliphate of `Uthman, prompted by the rapid spread of Islam, that a standard Qur'an was produced using the Qurayshi dialect and distributed to the main centers of the Islamic world. A few years later the Caliph Imam Ali began the codification of the rules concerning Arabic grammar and orthography. From there on numerous Islamic scholars have reviewed and excelled in all aspects of study related to the Qur'an, Allah's final and completed revelation.

Qur'anic science covers exegesis or commentary, its inimitability, the historical occasions for revelation of the verse, grammar, eloquence and readings. The names that are given to the Qur'an include: the Book (al-Kitab), the Discrimination (al-Furqan), the Guidance (al-Huda), the Remembrance (al-Dhikr) and others. The Qur'an reveals Allah's unity and attributes, prophethood, the return, the resurrection, the revealed code of conduct, numerous parables, prophecies, and sustainable guidelines for personal and social responsibility. Above all it illumines the way to freedom for the seeking mind and heart and dispels darkness and ignorance.

Reflection 2

Higher consciousness is only realizable by withdrawal from lower consciousness.

The Qur'an is the transcendent Word of the Transcendent Lord, Creator and Sustainer of all things. With it, creation began when Allah took our covenant with the soul of man with the question: "Am I not your Lord?"

The name 'Allah' is the ultimate Divine Name expressing Absolute Essence from which all attributes, names and manifestations emanate. Allah covers whatever is known, unknown, and cannot be covered or limited by creational indications. All great attributes, which we desire and seek, belong to Allah and yet none of these are the Essence. They are brought about and made manifest in meaning form by that all-Encompassing and yet apparently elusive but dominant and eternal Divine Presence. The most effulgent manifestation of Allah in our context is the Lord, the *Rabb*, of all kingdoms, within time and beyond it.

The path of *tawhīd*, Divine Oneness, begins with the intellect searching for the correspondence between outer events and actions. A subtler realm of unity is between attributes, such as the relationship between Beauty (ease) and Majesty (difficulty). Then comes the cosmic reality of unity in essence, One Source behind all the seen and the unseen. All human beings are driven along the path of *tawhīd* by the original primal desire for contentment/happiness. The Qur'an declares that it is only by remembrance of Allah that the heart becomes content (Surah *al-Ra`d* 13:28).

Exercise Three

"All human beings are driven along the path of **Tawhīd** *by the original primal desire for happiness. The Qur'an declares that it is only by remembrance of Allah that the heart becomes content"*

Reflect on the meaning of 'the Path of *Tawhīd*' in your life. For example, you could examine two areas of your life, such as family relationships, work, and friendships.

Reflection 3

Higher consciousness is only realizable by withdrawal from lower consciousness.

"The purpose of all creation is to know the Creator and follow His light by surrendering to it and living joyfully by it."

The Qur'an expounds on the ways of Allah which includes His Laws, His decrees and whatever governs the seen and unseen. The revealed knowledge of Allah also teaches us that He created all existence in pairs and opposites. Everything in existence is created in balance and rooted in its opposite; His decrees do not change, but destinies of individuals and societies change according to the path they choose to embark on.

Allah informs us in His book of the design and the basic human primal pattern that seeks the Eternal light and a state of paradise that all creation desires and adores Allah's attributes as He is the Source and Sustainer of all existence, and all things return to Him. It also tells us that Allah guides us to Him; that there is none other than Him. There is no god but Allah and Muhammad is His messenger.

The Qur'an teaches us that the entire cosmos is based on divine unity (*tawhīd*). He has designed all creation in a way that allows it to aspire to its highest potential and the making whole of everything is through submission to and a celebration of His eternal presence. In every circumstance He knows the right way to re-orientate anything towards Him. His decrees are all merciful and lead by Him to Him.

Reflection 4

Higher consciousness is only realizable by withdrawal from lower consciousness.

"The Qur'an unveils the way to Allah by Allah's mercy (*rahmah*) and equally identifies the cul-de-sac that draws us into confusion and destruction. It describes in detail the character, conduct and path of the believer and also the bleak picture of the non-believer. It highlights the pitfalls of the ego-self (nafs) and how one may sublimate and transform into an enlightened being."

Although the Qur'an is a treasury of information, its real glory and miracle lie in its power to transform those who approach it with faith and the conviction that it is the revealed divine blueprint. It unveils itself and clarifies what appears to be obscure in some parts by other sections within it. The organic interrelationship of all its topics reflects reality in such a way that it defies a purely structural or scholastic approach. As the manifestation of the highest godly attributes in human form, the Prophet Muhammad was described as the 'living Qur'an'.

He considered all prophets and messengers his brothers. Indeed, he considered all mankind to be a single brotherhood, all men and women being equal in the eyes of the Creator. Those most honored by the Creator are those who are humble and sincere in their submission to Him, irrespective of gender or social status.

During his stay in Mecca after Allah declared him a prophet, the Prophet Muhammad only spoke about Allah. He recited from the Qur'an what Allah desired of His creation, what pleased Him and the ways in which people could potentially be distracted from Him. The Qur'anic message revealed during the 13 years of the Meccan period focuses on self-enlightenment based on selfless action and reflection.

Foundations – Charting the Way – Map No. 5: The Qur'anic Prescription for Life

- Qur'anic Revealed Knowledge – Qur'anic Prescription for Life

- Relevant Prophetic Teachings – Qur'anic Prescription for Life

Qur'anic Revealed Knowledge – Qur'anic Prescription for Life

Allah says:

> "If We caused this Qur'an to descend upon a mountain, you would have seen it humbled and coming apart from fear of Allah. And these examples We present to the people that perhaps they will give thought." (Surah *al-Hashr* 59:21)

> "Alif Lam Mim! *This is the book; in it there is no doubt. It is guidance for those in awareness (*taqwa*). Those who have faith (*iman*) in the unseen, establish prayer (*salat*), and spend of what We have bestowed upon them, And who have faith in that which has been sent down to you and what was sent down before you, and are certain about the Hereafter (*Akhirah*). They follow guidance from their Lord. They are the successful."* (Surah *al-Baqarah* 2:2-5)

Relevant Prophetic Teachings – Qur'anic Prescription for Life

1. "Exalt yourself with the Book of Allah, for surely it is a strong rope, and a clear light, and a beneficial cure, and a thirst-quenching source, and a protection for those who hold fast to it and a source of freedom for those who cling to it."
2. Nobody sits down with this Qur'an without having experienced either an increase or a decrease when he stands up again: an increase in guidance, or a decrease in 'blindness'.

Charting the Way – Map No. 5: Exercises to Deepen Learning

(The Qur'anic Prescription for Life)

Title:
What is the importance and purpose of the Qur'an for human beings?

Word Length:
Between 500 and 1000 words.

Criteria:
You may find the following criteria useful in addressing the question:

1. The meaning & purpose of 'Divine Revelation'.
2. Qur'anic explanation of the patterns & purpose of existence.
3. Qur'anic teachings about both outer transactions and the inner spiritual dimensions (e.g., teachings about the self, soul and spiritual practices).
4. You may use examples from your experience, or the experience of others.

Charting the Way – Map No. 5: Multiple Choice Quiz
(The Qur'anic Prescription for Life)

*The purpose of the quiz is for you to test your own understanding of this map. Choose the **BEST** answer A, B, C, or D:*

Questions:

Q 1: The <u>main</u> benefit of the Qur'anic message (approached correctly) for the individual is
   A. S/He will be purified if s/he reads it regularly
   B. S/He will be transformed and awakened
   C. S/He will understand and follow *Shari`ah*
   D. S/He will avoid pitfalls of the lower self

Q 2: 'Transformation' means
   A. An ordinary person becoming a Prophet
   B. Changing one's behavior from vice to virtue
   C. Reaching a state of inner contentment &submission
   D. Giving up bad habits

Q 3: The only way to achieve contentment is
   A. Following the primal desire for happiness
   B. Recognizing the unity of creation
   C. Personal and social responsibility
   D. Constant remembrance of Allah

Q 4: The Prophet was called the 'living Qur'an' because
   A. He knew it by heart
   B. No-one else received the revelation
   C. He obeyed its commands
   D. He was the highest human manifestation of Divine attributes

Answers:
   1: B.
   2: C.
   3: D.
   4: D.

CHARTING THE WAY – MAP NO. 6: Acts of Worship

This map corresponds to Lesson SIX of ASK Course TWO. In this map we are shown the vital link between acts of worship and a heightening in our awareness of the divine.

Charting the Way: Map No. 6 – Contents

- Learning Objectives
- Overview
- Charting the Way – Map No. 6: Acts of Worship
    * Submission
    * The Call from Within
    * Reality
    * How Outer Restrictions Lead to Inner Expansion
    * The Rituals
    * Accessing the Light
    * Worship and Community
- Reflection 1
- Reflection 2
- Foundations – Charting the Way – Map No. 6: Acts of Worship
    * Qur'anic Revealed Knowledge – Acts of Worship
    * Relevant Prophetic Teachings – Acts of Worship
- Exercises / Multiple Choice Quiz

Learning Objectives

From this map, you will gain an understanding of:

1. All actions emanate from a need or desire to improve our state.
2. The prescribed acts of worship in the *dīn* help us regulate our lives and thoughts so we may enhance our awareness and gain access to higher consciousness.
3. While outer rituals and acts of worship form a major part of all religions, the rituals of Islam are pristine and have their roots in its inner spiritual cosmology, and are a call to us from the inner recesses of our soul.
4. Such acts of worship acknowledge the Source of creation: the Divine Presence is the only Being worthy of worship and our life itself is the only altar upon which we worship.
5. Acts of worship connect a personal and individual practice to that of the community and to society at large.

Overview

All outer acts of worship in all religions must help a person to arrive at a deep understanding of inner meanings and the true purpose underlying such acts; otherwise, they remain empty rituals bereft of meaning. Worship is the ultimate demonstration of a person's adoration and love for the object of worship, who, in the case of this Course, is nothing less than the One Source of everything. The yearning to worship is ingrained within our soul. By performing the ritual acts of worship, we are attempting to unify our mind, body and actions to work together with the Divine attributes that are so deeply loved and desired. All ritual worship, in effect, is an attempt to be in unison with Divine consciousness.

Charting the Way – Map No. 6: Acts of Worship

Essentially all our actions are motivated by a need or a desire to act which we hope will make our condition better than it is. They are undertaken as attempts to improve our state or to prevent our situation from deteriorating. Whether it is an action motivated purely by worldly needs and desires or by a genuinely spiritual yearning, the ultimate aim is always contentment and a move away from agitation.

In the case of acts of worship our hope rests on the possibility that by doing a certain ritual our future state will be better than it is now and that this newly achieved state will be more content, stable, balanced and tranquil, because that is our innate condition.

The challenge is that acts of worship sometimes seem to lack efficacy because they may be done without direction on the one hand and lack clarity about whom or what is being worshipped on the other.

There is no possibility for an act to occur unless it is based on love and desire, but it may be a muddled kind of love, not clearly oriented towards the Divine Presence. Acts of worship ought to be acts that express our love and passion for what is most worthy of our love and adoration. Since man was created to worship (Surah *al-Dhariyat* 51:56) he cannot but worship, and so every human act is, in a sense, an act of worship.

However, unless it is performed with the awareness of who is being worshipped, it may be completely misdirected.

In such a case the purpose of the divinely intended worship and thus the raison d'être of the worshipper are both defeated and may even lead to the abomination of idolatry.

Submission

In order to align my outer ritual worship with what is prescribed for my well-being on an inner level I have to be in submission to a greater absolute truth, which is *islam* – submission to the truth. Submission to the truth means submission to oneness, to wholeness: I want to be fulfilled, I need to be content, I desire to be happy. I submit to the fact that I need knowledge and that I am not happy with ignorance. So, I submit to the truth of my innermost reality and such submission leads me to a deep sense of contentment. My submission cuts through all other distractions and desires and takes me to a singular point of focus.

My contentment is based on modesty and saying 'enough is enough' and I submit to the fact that I only have access to the truth in the 'now', in the current moment. I have no access to yesterday; it is gone. I have no knowledge about the outcomes tomorrow will bring. So, tomorrow is an expectation that may never happen or be grasped. I may get the wealth I am looking for tomorrow but with it I may also end up inwardly bereft. So, the outcome may be dreadful even though I achieve what I have been longing for.

I submit to the truth that my only connection with absolute truth, *haqq*, is now. Therefore, I am a slave of the moment – *abdul waqt*. Not that I belong to or worship time, but that the present moment is my only opportunity to submit, to worship and thus to truly 'be'.

I also submit to the truth that I want to know the source of all these qualities that I desire (patience, generosity, compassion, power and so on). I submit to the fact that I am starting with ignorance and am hopeful that I will come to know. Where does that source of knowledge come from? It's already there within me.

The Call from Within

Conscious acts of worship are essentially ways in which to regulate our lives and thoughts and improve our skills at different levels of awareness and consciousness. As a result, we may become aware of how many times we are distracted–in *ghaflah*. Acts of worship are programs of reconstruction and a reaffirmation of our covenant from pre-creation. They have been established to help us discover the gaps of forgetfulness as we go through life's ups and downs and also to bring to our attention any disconnectedness between our inner state and the light within us. For example, *Salat*, the act of prayer, stops us from being forgetful and prevents us from causing harm to ourselves and to others (Surah *Ta Ha* 20:14).

When we 'neutralize' ourselves in this way by performing *salat* we are caught up less in the worldly dynamic that so often threatens to distract us from the remembrance of Oneness. Then we remember the original Light, the higher. Allah is the highest *'wala dhikrullahi akbar'*[6]. This remembrance then delimits our consciousness of worldly affairs and increases our consciousness of spiritual affairs.

All religious disciplines seemingly begin their program in the outer but are in fact driven by a call from the inner. The worshiper is expressing himself/herself to the object of his/her worship in this way: "I come to you with this physical act as an expression of my inner love for you which you have embedded in my soul. If I do not express my love for you with a physical act of worship to match my inner yearning, my worship is incomplete."

If a ritual act of worship is not undertaken one way or another, the worshiper is not expressing his or her love for the Creator in a complete and holistic way. It has to have an outer form because we are manifest creatures caught in space and time.

---

[6] "and the remembrance of Allah is greater than anything you can possibly conceive of"

Reality

Submission to the truth is the natural state of any intelligent human; the realization that I am not totally independent, this is true submission. I submit to the truth that I am totally dependent for my tranquility on other factors. These other factors may sometimes be an intrinsic part of my innate nature or exogenous to it but never separate from it. So, I accept I have no complete power of my own. The only power I have is to adore and worship and that in itself brings about change within and without.

To worship means to focus on the ultimate Reality and Truth – *al Haqq* – and the more focused I am the more my perception will be attuned to reality so that deception and illusion no longer have a hold on me and I begin to see things as they are.

If I see things as they are then my actions will always be appropriate to any situation that may arise. That is why he who sees what is as it is – *insan al kamil (see also Map 2)* has only one option to act. If we recall, the definition of *insan al kamil*, the universal or perfect man (perfect in the sense of having perfected one's perception and action) is indicated in the Qur'an: *"Say: 'Truly, my prayer and my offering and my life and my death are for Allah, the Sustainer Lord of all realms of existence"* (Surah al-An`am 6:162).

As *insan al kamil* I cannot act differently because I am seeing things as they are and my task, my life, my existence is based on trying to maintain that balance as best I can. This is demonstrated sometimes by my words and sometimes by my silence, sometimes through stillness, sometimes through action.

All acts of worship, their meanings and their effects on an individual and the society he or she inhabits are interconnected. The path of Islam relates to the seen and the unseen, intention and action and the inseparable relationship between the Creator and creation. Every ritual that we perform in Islam has several levels of meaning and also has specific effects on us. It is assumed that students are already familiar with the form and rules of each obligatory ritual act. Here follows a brief summary of the main rituals and some of their deeper meanings. (*Adapted from* "Inner meanings of Worship in Islam" *by Shaykh Fadhlalla Haeri*).

Exercise One – Focusing and Submitting

*I submit to the truth that my only connection with Truth (*haqq*) is in the now.*

After discussion with a wise person, make a list of practices which can help you to be 'in the now'. Which of these practices helps you the most?

How Outer Restrictions Lead to Inner Expansion

All forms of worship play a pivotal part in the perfection and maintenance of man's inner and outer equilibrium. These acts and rituals have been given to mankind as part of the universally established balance within creation, which is a facet of Divine justice.

The equilibrium within man, like in all other limited creatures, subjects the pairs of opposites which they are composed of to a dynamic interplay: an increase in quantity results in a decrease in quality; an increase in size and form tends to lead to a decrease in substance and meaning; a decrease in the subtle inner increases the influence of the ego-self and therefore decreases the self's connectedness to the soul, and so forth.

For example, the outer world and the senses are given precedence over all else by a child developing naturally, and rightly so. But with progressing life experience and age, wisdom develops and a mature and healthy person will naturally be drawn to subtler meanings and unseen patterns while retaining earthly wisdom. Every act of worship makes us more aware of the dynamics of outer restraint, leading to inner expansion and thus sets this natural direction: to move from the *dunya* (the world) to the *akhirah* (afterlife) – from the transient to the permanent.

The Rituals

Shahadah (The Creed)

The proclamation and deep consciousness of "There is no God but Allah and Muhammad is the messenger of Allah" forms the foundation of the *din*. The path of enlightenment is rooted in the truth that Allah is the only source of life, and the truth that the human being is the pinnacle of all manifest creation and potentially Allah's representative in this world.

Wudu (Ablution)

> *"Wudu performed over wudu is light upon light"* – Prophet Muhammad

With ablution (*wudu*) we aim to focus our intention towards a single action, centering ourselves into the present moment and sealing our minds and hearts against the negative impacts of the world.

Washing the two hands signifies abandoning all things that have a hold on us, whether it is possessions or ideas or a self-image while washing the face symbolizes, amongst many things, cleansing the heart of attachment to worldly desires.

Wiping the head shows that we are maintaining our higher, rational faculties of reasoning and will not succumb to the promptings of our ego-self.

Wiping the feet reminds us that our steps must only lead us to Allah and that we must rein in our inner drives.

The use of water has a naturally purifying and calming effect and the turning inward of our attention completes the preparation for rising to the highest potential within us in prayer, *salat*.

Salat (Prayer)

> *"Those in faith are successful who are humble in their prayer"*
> (Surah *al-Mu'minum* 23:1)

The primary act of worship in Islam is the prayer, *salat*. The prayer comprises many elements, each with its rich inner meaning.

The Qur'an enjoins all the faithful to *"keep up prayer; surely prayer is a timed ordinance for the believers"* (Surah *al-Nisa* 4:103). Muslims base their prayers on the prophetic practice of five prayers during the three periods of the day: daybreak; noon and mid afternoon, after sunset and at night.

The Qur'an describes those who are faithful as being in a perpetual state of salat (Surah *al-Ma`arij* 70:23). It is not the ritual itself that is implied here but what the performance of such a ritual imparts to the person: inner serenity and the correct orientation.

Salat 'recharges' us and reaffirms our faith based as it is on inner stillness and silence contained within specified outer movements. Performed in congregation it joins individuals into a uniform whole, each person equal in the eyes of the Creator. The individual who performs *salat* is outwardly and inwardly cleansed. He relinquishes his management of affairs of the world and calls for help and support from the Creator of the seen and unseen. In the act of prayer, we return to our roots through bending and bowing, as do other animals, and then disappearing into the earth as do all plants and the most basic of earthly creatures. Done in the correct way and with the right intention, *salat* is the gateway to the knowledge of Allah's attributes.

The intention (*niyyah*) at the outset of the prayer is made to eliminate *shirk* (literally, associating partners with Allah) with the aim of removing both external idols and the idols that we generate within ourselves, like conceit, pride and ostentation, or our fears and false expectations. On a deeper level our sincere intention has the power to help us focus only on the Divine and not on our ego-self.

The *salat* begins with the declaration that God is greater or beyond anything we can comprehend, logically understand or conceptualize. Raising up the hands with open palms signifies that the seeker has relinquished everything he/she has owned, owns, or will own, and given up all illusions of possessing power and authority independent of Allah, while saying the *takbir* – *Allahu Akbar*.

With this *takbir* and the subsequently repeated ones along with all the invocations in the prayer, we are awestruck by Divine Majesty and hope to remain unwavering in being transfixed by His splendor. We praise Him and express our gratitude to Him, reaffirm our dependence and seek guidance and protection from Him. In the standing position (*qiyam*) we are ready to fulfill our obligations in this world and in the hereafter, head bowed in humility, accepting all our faults and shortcomings and visualizing ourselves in the divine court of the physical and spiritual realms. So begins an intimate dialogue between this apparently separate entity (the human being) and the majestic Truth that encompasses everything.

Bowing from the waist in *ruku'*, we praise the Creator with utter humility and sincerely express our gratitude, and this is, we are assured, heard. The bending symbolizes our fall from any state we may be attached to or imagine we have achieved; turning away from everything that distracts us from our Source.

The pinnacle of the prayer is the *sajda*, prostration, which some traditions say signifies our return to the building-blocks of our creation, the dust of the earth. It represents the shutting down of all our senses and, in that lowliest of positions, also our highest potential as consciously submitted creatures who willingly acknowledge their non-existence.

If we want to be at the threshold of the original Light then we must disappear from all shadowy lights, the ego-self. That is how we move up the scale of consciousness, from personal awareness through the transcendental steps towards the ever-present and Supreme Consciousness.

Exercise Two – Purpose of *Salat*

After reading the section on *salat*, revisit Exercise One and consider again how you can **'move up the scale of consciousness….towards the ever-present and Supreme Consciousness'**

Sawm (Fasting)

> *"Everything has a door and the door to acts of devotion is fasting"* – Prophet Muhammad

Fasting was practiced in all those communities that had a messenger or prophet. The fast described in the Qur'an involves abstinence from all intake of food or drink from dawn to sunset during one specific month of the year, Ramadan, the ninth month of the Muslim year. The Prophet Muhammad fasted regularly throughout the year and recommended that all Muslims should do so. During the last years of his life, it is known that he fasted for at least three days in every month.

The benefits of the fast are numerous, ranging from the physiological to the mental and spiritual, and aim to bring about greater awareness and sensitivity towards oneself and creation.

While keeping the fast it is necessary to abstain from sexual intercourse as well as other sensory excitement or distraction. Fasting entails not listening to or engaging in slander, and refraining from anger and all other vices. One must behave in such a considered way that one acts only to please Allah.

Apart from outer abstinence, we need to take heed of what is concealed within our inner desires and drives, and use the clarity the fast brings to weed out anything that will block consciousness of our Source. Of all the ritual acts of worship the fast is a secret between the worshiper and the worshiped (see also Surah *al-Baqarah* 2:183).

In a Sacred Tradition it is stated that fasting is undertaken purely for Him. In this respect the practice of fasting forms a bridge between formal worship and our profound inner transformation. A reduction in physical, mental and other desires and concerns enables a closer connection of the self to the soul. The act of fasting entails purification at numerous levels so that the ever-present pure light within the heart overflows into the human being and into his/her surroundings.

Fasting from unnecessary speech, from looking at things that will generate overwhelming desires, from hearing gossip and slander and those who seek to mislead by their words, from smelling scents both pleasant and foul, acquiring a 'taste' for unfair gain of any sort over those weaker than ourselves and reaching out and touching something that will once more cause us to veer towards imbalance and disharmony, all negate the fast.

Being abstemious naturally leads to a deeper form of restraint that reaches the inner senses. Through the fast we hope to learn to turn our intellect and faculty of reasoning away from narrow worldly interests to a healthy balance of inner and outer where the natural limits are preserved and we do no harm to ourselves or to others.

We try through our clear reasoning powers brought about by fasting to be mindful of our *khayal*, or the inner sense of imagination within us, without letting it run away into the realms of fantasy. While the inner sense of imagination has its place in perceiving subtle unseen concepts and understanding what underpins the world of matter, it can also lead us away from the truth if not curbed.

The fast also provides an opportunity to restrain the force of illusion or the way in which we attribute meaning and value to an event, known as *wahm*. This is also an important inner sense when it is used with the correct degree of reasoning. If not, *wahm* tosses us around between love and hate, anger and lust and stops us from being steadfast on the path of balance and unity.

We have been granted the facility to process the messages that these inner and outer senses send us at every moment and filter out those that are harmful to us, and in this way the fasting worshiper, stripped of everything but his/her devotion to the One, can truly witness the One inwardly and outwardly.

Zakat (Charity or Tax)

"You will never attain to righteousness until you spend of what you love." (Surah ale-'Imran 3:96)

Charity or alms-giving is obligatory for every Muslim. Traditionally *zakat* has been a tax levied on a certain quantity of specific commodities, such as wheat, barley, dates, livestock, and so on. When a threshold in the quantity of these goods is exceeded then *zakat* becomes obligatory.

Often taken to mean simply 'tax' or 'alms', *zakat* also means growth, increase, nearness, goodness and purification. In this latter sense, *zakat* is very much like pruning a tree, for example, where the excess foliage is cut off, which in turn results in an increase in the yield of fruit.

Zakat is imitating in our small way the attribute of the almighty, Giver. Allah owns and gives all that there is, known and unknown, and as true slaves of Allah we too must reflect this quality, hopefully shedding our miserliness and greed along the way.

There are numerous levels of *zakat*, starting with the obligatory *shari'ah* injunction, which covers all Muslims, and moves towards giving away even what you want to keep.

As noted above, the root of the word *zakat* means to purify, and what really needs to be purified is my ego-self and my image of it, which is formed in my mind. Giving up all that is transient leaves us with only the purity of the soul, which is the ultimate gift and treasure.

The recipients of *zakat* are also specified as the poor, the needy, and travelers in the way of Allah who enhance the *din* by their words and deeds. It is therefore the duty of every Muslim to share what they have been given of wealth, time, and other skills and resources in order to care for all humanity and all creation.

Exercise Three – Purification

Think back to the last time you fasted or gave *zakat*. How did these acts purify you? If you feel they did not, why do you think that was the case?

Hajj (the Pilgrimage)

> *"We shall show them Our signs on the horizons and in their souls so that the truth will become clear to them"* (Surah *Ha Mim* 41:53)

The Arabs have performed a ritual pilgrimage around the Ka`bah in the sacred precinct in the city of Makkah from time immemorial. Christians, Jews and many others also brought their offerings and joined in circling (*tawaf*) the Ka`bah. The Prophet Muhammad performed the full Islamic *Hajj* only once in his lifetime shortly before his passing. The word literally means 'endeavor, aspiration, intention, destination, object, goal, aim'.

Apart from the many spiritual benefits to the individual, the Hajj is also a powerful symbol of the social, cultural and political marketplace. It is here that all Muslims meet, greet, interact and embrace each other. The physical and heavenly point of unity, the Black Stone, witnesses and records their parting kiss. *Hajj* has always greatly influenced the life of all Muslims for it brings together a powerful mass of people with the express purpose of abandoning this world in pursuit of the knowledge of the Creator of this world. *Hajj* thus links the whole of the Muslim world. It is both a personal migration and an acknowledgement of mankind's sameness as well as its diversity. It reminds Muslims that irrespective of color, culture or any other differences, they all seek salvation and a confirmation of the Divine Presence in their lives.

After much effort and leaving behind what has been accumulated in worldly terms, the individual performing the *Hajj* leaves with only the most basic covering, similar to a burial shroud, to gather with the multitudes on the dusty plains of Arafat, to supplicate and declare his or her bereft state. If the self and personality is truly bereft, then the soul is paramount.

The significance of the story of the Prophet Abraham is clearly re-enacted with the aim of absorbing it and applying its principles in our lives. The Prophet Abraham had only one attachment and love in his heart, which was for his son, Ismail. A miraculous event occurred and he had to abandon this attachment by a willingness to sacrifice Ismail.

Once that equally profound but ultimately earthly love was made subservient to the higher, this all-encompassing Divine love permeated existence giving rise to the manifestation of the ram, which was sacrificed instead of Ismail.

In all its complex profundity, the *Hajj* is ultimately a declaration of total abandonment on the part of the worshiper and the realization of the zone of Divine abundance within and around him/her.

Exercise Four – Abandonment of the Self

Hajj is ultimately a declaration of total abandonment... and the realization of the zone of divine abundance around the individual.

If you have been on *Hajj*, consider to what extent you were in this state at the time.

If you have not been on *Hajj*, consider one single thing you could do to prepare for it.

Jihad (Struggle in the Service of God)

> *"Your greatest enemy is your ego-self, which is within you."* – Prophet Muhammad

If we look at the fundamentals of existence, science tells us that all life manifests due to complex interactions between energy and matter, and every living creature, from the smallest and simplest amoeba to the complex human being, enacts this constant interchange and movement at every seen and unseen level. Life exists as bundles of energy, forming and disintegrating. The root of the word *jihad* originates from *juhd*, which means 'energy', so in a sense all of creation is in *jihad*, knowingly or otherwise.

Striving, struggling and doing one's best in order to achieve a worthy objective are all necessary conditions for human improvement and development. Enjoined upon all Muslims, *jihad* has a hierarchy starting from the greater *jihad*, which is monitoring one's ego-self and one's lower tendencies, to the lesser *jihad* which is defending one's community against unlawful attack and persecution and dealing equitably within one's society.

Priority is given to the greater *jihad*, which involves self-purification that will lead to correct inspiration and guidance from within – a prelude to a greater awakening and ultimately to enlightenment. Then one may turn to striving and struggle in relation to the outer world, which includes helping others, teaching, improving social conditions and so on. It may also include a willingness to put one's life in danger when the circumstances demand it. *Jihad* involves struggling by whatever means at our disposal towards the ultimate purpose for which we have been created.

The two kinds of *jihad* interact with and lead to each other and are not by any means meant to be mutually exclusive. Much of outer *jihad* and good actions are undertaken in order to discover and experience a better or higher state, while the inner *jihad* helps us cast aside the ego-self and bask in the effulgence of the soul in the heart.

Amr bil Ma`ruf wan-Nahi an-il Munkir (Enjoining Good and Forbidding Evil)

> *"Do you command people to righteousness and forget yourselves?"* (Surah *al-Baqarah* 2:44)

Encouraging goodness and forbidding evil is part of the social fabric and foundation of any civilization. This enjoinder implies that the individual already practicing these virtues must remind others and transmit to them this civilized form of behavior so that society as a whole may be positively influenced. It is also a part of *jihad*.

In order to meet the requirements of this obligatory act of worship there are a number of stipulations, some of which are listed very briefly here:

1. That the person forbidding and enjoining is well-versed in what is right and wrong.
2. That he/she must follow this guidance and apply it to him/herself.
3. That he/she must not have any hidden motivation when telling people what is incorrect or correct.
4. That he/she must be merciful, kind and sensitive in his/her dealings.
5. That he/she recognizes people's behavior and state and speaks to them in a way that they will understand.
6. That he/she should be patient with hostility shown towards him/her and must not be vengeful or fanatical.
7. That the intention is to please only Allah and to trust in His judgment.
8. To continually examine his/her own shortcomings and when commanding others, to check that he/she begins with him/herself.

Exercise Five – *Jihad* and *Amr bil Ma`ruf*

*"Most of outer **jihad** and good actions are to discover and experience a better or higher state. As for inner **jihad** it is to cast aside the self and bask in the effulgence of the soul in the heart."*

What outer and inner *jihad* is going on in your life at the moment and how do they relate to each other?

Accessing the Light

The way to Absolute Light is via a range of modified lights. The soul is exposed to the spectrum of Divine attributes that crisscross the spheres of time and space as energy beams. Every soul knows and loves these Divine attributes.

Love of Allah is indeed the love of these attributes and to know Allah is through living these Divine attributes. This is one of the higher realizations of the prophetic tradition, *man `arafa nafsahu qad `arafa rabbah,* "He who knows himself, knows his Lord".

All religious paths attempt this transformation and the resurrection from self to soul, from worldly limitations to the boundless that is found beyond the horizon of these attributes. Thus, whatever we like or admire – eternal ongoing, beauty, majesty, wealth, and so on – we are actually praising an aspect of the Creator. The dark shadows of these attributes appear when worship is misdirected or perverted. This happens, for example, when we allow our ego-self to misappropriate those Divine attributes and ascribe them to ourselves; when we fall prey to the illusion that we possess all power, majesty, beauty and so on and then act in an unjust and arrogant manner.

Acts of worship also point towards and acknowledge the source of creation and our life itself becomes an altar upon which we worship. The wholesome growth of an individual moves from its biological and physiological phases to the development of mind and intellect and then the evolved heart. There is a natural progression for human beings to start with only physical concerns and grow towards the realization that the physical as well as the non-physical, the form and the meaning, have all been directed towards the Source of creation and the Sustainer to whom everything eventually returns. That is one of the higher meanings of *la ilaha illa 'llah*[7].

If you see other than the One, this too is part of the mercy of the One. The original light is veiled by many veils which also contain His mercy within them.[8] The sincere seeker will see mercy even in constriction and difficulty. This is not only due to an unswerving faith on his or her part but by actually experiencing the benefits of being in a state of conscious submission. So, he/she naturally praises and glorifies the One in every state.

Worship and Community

Acts of worship in Islam are divided into those that are obligatory and others that are supererogatory or extra. The obligatory acts are further categorized into individual obligations (*fard al `ayn*) and collective ones (*fard*

---

[7] *"There is no god except Allah!"*
[8] This is what is meant by the Sacred Tradition: *"The vastness of My Mercy covers everything"*, and since He is the Inward and the Outward, the envelope of His Mercy is also from within and from without.

al kifayah) – which means the obligation is fulfilled if a part of the community fulfills it, but where each member of the community is answerable if none of them fulfill it.

Although your ultimate reality is that you are alone with your Lord every act of worship is also connected with the social environment you are in, whether in its execution, for example, prayer in congregation, the obligatory fast, or the pilgrimage and so on, or in its effect, like the circulation of wealth in the distribution of mandatory and voluntary charity. Personal and individual practice is in this way linked to society and community.

There is a wonderful and dynamic interplay between individual and collective obligations in the performance of acts of worship. Whatever is in existence is balanced by its complementary opposite and when that relationship is properly established then stability on a personal and social level becomes evident. When individual practices of worship are performed collectively a firm foundation for a community is laid down. The beneficial effects of companionship, of mirroring and witnessing many individuals who are on the path become a habit. It is then that a community with solidarity begins to grow. Collective worship enhances the personal benefits gained from worship and vice versa.

So, Islam has universalized and re-crystallized the collective prophetic consciousness and packaged it as a way of life; a foundation based on divine revelation and knowledge from which a cohesive community may design itself. Islam is the art of submission to Allah, who is in control of all existence. It is the acknowledgement of our personal and collective submission and surrender to the One, after which we must learn how to correctly interact with our world of change and uncertainty.

Reflection 1

Higher consciousness is only realizable by withdrawal from lower consciousness.

"Essentially all our actions are motivated by a need or a desire to act which we hope will make our condition better than it is. They are attempts to improve our state or to prevent our situation from deteriorating."

Desire arises from a perceived sense of lack or dissatisfaction with our current lot in life. Our natural state is one of wholeness and fulfillment and any such perceived or real lack gives rise to discontentment and a subsequent desire to redress the imbalance. So being discontent is a power that motivates us. It spurs us on; it pushes us towards action. The Prophet Muhammad has said: "O man, you are struggling all the time, struggling in order to know your Lord". So, the root of desire, the root of our discontent, is a power that is genetically encoded within us.

Desire is like a fire; the more we fan it the more it will burn and the more powerfully it will rage. It exists in order to take us to the ultimate goal of self-knowledge or to the brink of disappointment and to the edge of despair.

Hope is the desire to bring about harmony, peace and connectedness, inwardly and outwardly. All hope is related to trying to stop something that causes disharmony or creating a new element that brings about increased harmony. Hope and expectation are strongly connected. Expectation is related to what can be achieved; the fulfillment of expectation can be planned for concretely. The levels of hope vary with its object. Someone hopes for health and physical well-being; another hopes for awakening to Reality beyond the physical world.

If the two desires are aligned there is greater likelihood of wholesomeness and success.

Reflection 2

Higher consciousness is only realizable by withdrawal from lower consciousness.

Submission or surrender (islam) implies that even though I have submitted to the truth, any pain or physical constraint will take momentary precedence over my desire for lofty spiritual knowledge. I may tell you that all I want is to know the qualities of Allah but if there is a sudden pain in my toe, I will forget all of that and be conscious of nothing other than my toe. So, I am forced to submit to that fleeting reality. In this way we experience submission in its totality, not partially. Submission to the truth is freedom from falsehood. Otherwise, I may just be another pompous person trying to appear pious and telling everyone, 'I am a man of Allah'.

All of the beings of light/prophets are under the aegis of the same laws of the Creator. The Prophet Muhammad and other enlightened beings before and after him have had to submit to the same laws of existence as all creation. As a matter of fact, the secret and essence of their greatness lies in the perfection of their `abdiyah, i.e., the very humility of submitting to the laws and etiquette of the realm in which they find themselves at every moment, irrespective of the fact that they may have access to much higher states of divine intimacy than the average man or woman.

Iman is the response to the Creator's call by the person in the state of submission- *islam*.[9] S/he knows with absolute certainty that there is something innate

---

[9] Surah *ale `Imran* 3:193: *"Our Lord! We have heard the call of one calling (us) to Faith, 'Believe in your Lord', and we have believed ..."*

that is beyond all of these changes and beyond all of these needs. We only know our needs because within us there is a zone that has no needs and it is called the soul. Access to our soul is through our heart. The way our heart comes to life and gives us this access is by us avoiding giving all our time and nourishment to our ego-self. We only have a certain amount of time and energy that needs to be used wisely. If we feed the weeds (the whims and desires of the ego-self) they will grow strong and hamper the growth of the main plants which produce the fruit and the sweet fragrance we so love (the virtues).

The main plant is the heart *qalb*. So, the entire business of faith and action, which leads to perfection, *ihsan*, is to ensure that the heart is fulfilled in order for it to bear fruit. *Ihsan* means the most beautiful, the most perfect thing. Enlightenment is the by-product of the growth, development and enrichment of the heart. The fruit of faith -*iman*- is that you know whatever situation you are in is brought about by the perfect designs of the perfect Creator. After that you can only act with *ihsan* because *ihsan* has been done to you. Once it is done to you, it will overflow from you. You cannot help it overflowing and emanating from you.

Islam is submission to the truth at all its levels, at all the layers of consciousness, for example, submission to our lower level of consciousness, to our mind's consciousness, to our heart's consciousness, to our *rūh*'s consciousness. Automatically we submit to our vegetative consciousness even though we are not aware of it — everything is fulfilling its function.

There is no end to these layers of consciousness. They form within us as teachers, as parents, as memories, or any roles we may take on in our lives. These are all different facets or reflections of that light of the intellect emanating from the *rūh*, and the cumulative perception of these reflections is what we call consciousness. It is a means to *iman*.

The more we train our perception the keener becomes its penetration and signs become apparent that 'there is more than meets the eye'; that there is not only the visible – *dhahir* – but also the invisible – *batin*; not only worldly but also heavenly. Then I start to be balanced. My consciousness becomes more attuned with pure consciousness as and when I need to access it.

Whatever I may be conscious of, be it anger or anything else, is referred to pure consciousness and emerges in a manner that is appropriate, that is comprehensible and coherent.

So, in summary, Islam is submitting to the truth of all the situations that we find ourselves in. *Iman* is the knowledge that none of these are anything other than the shadows or reflections from the original template of our inner, pure consciousness. *Ihsan* is the realization of this knowledge and its translation into action. Such action is not guided by whims and desires any more but by correct knowledge. We cannot do better than what we are doing because we are acting from pure consciousness. This is what is meant by the famous prophetic tradition "…to worship Allah as if you see Him, and if you cannot see Him, you know that He sees you…"

Exercise Six – The Truth and Pure Consciousness

"Islam is submitting to the truth of all the situations that you are in. Iman is the knowledge that none of these are anything other than the shadows or reflections of the original template of your inner pure consciousness."

Reflect on the meaning of this statement in relation to any difficult situation.

Foundations – Charting the Way – Map No. 6: Acts of Worship

- Qur'anic Revealed Knowledge – Acts of Worship

- Relevant Prophetic Teachings – Acts of Worship

Qur'anic Revealed Knowledge – Acts of Worship

Apart from the clearly restricted actions and prohibitions, there is much freedom of choice and many worldly pleasures that the seeker can enjoy. What we experience of this world is but a small sample or prelude of what is to come in the Hereafter. Outer forms perceived through the senses are only doors to meanings and the recognition of attributes. We realize that all worldly existence is founded on opposite qualities balancing each other and yet rooted in one another. The only constant reference point is the perfection of the One.

Correct transactions and a proper relationship with creation are essential for spiritual progress. The truth is that all humankind has emerged from the One, original, primal soul. However, as individuals, we are different in terms of our looks, biology, as well as states of consciousness and cultures.

Virtuous and moral conduct is essential for the inner health of the seeker of truth. A sound knowledge of the Qur'an and the teachings of the Messenger are essential for safe passage through life. Outer limitations and laws are necessary preparations for inner illumination and relief and are also very important for our protection.[10]

Allah says:

> "O you who believe, enter Islam completely, and do not follow the bidding of Shaytan. Indeed, he is your open enemy." (Surah al-Baqarah 2/208)

> "O you who have faith, bow down, prostrate yourselves, worship your Lord, and do good so that hopefully you may prosper. Strive for Allah with the endeavor that is due to Him. He has chosen you and not placed any hardships upon you in the religion. It is the faith of your father Abraham. He has named you Muslims before and now so that the messenger maybe a witness upon you and that you may be witnesses against mankind. So, establish prayer, pay the alms tax and hold fast to Allah. He is your Protector, the best Protector-and a blessed helper." (Surah al-Hajj 77-78)

---

[10] The role of *Shaytan* in Creation is – as far as it concerns us – that of the antagonist to man (man and jinn have been identified in Surah *al-Rahman* and many other places as one of the creational pairs of opposites/complements) and in fulfillment of this role, he has been given certain powers over man, but only if man falls short in sincerity [Surah *al-Hijr* 15/39-42 and other places]. Sincerity and purity in intention are inward qualities but in order to perfect them they require an outward manifestation, and outer laws and limitations provide the platform for it.

Relevant Prophetic Teachings – Acts of Worship

1. "There are three kinds of worship; people who worship Allah in fear, they are the slaves; people who worship for reward – they are paid slaves, and those who worship Allah out of love for Him–these are freed slaves, and this is the best kind of worship."
2. "The most beloved people of Allah are those whose hands are the most generous, and the most generous people are those who pay *zakat* from their wealth and are not niggardly with the believers concerning their wealth and what Allah has made obligatory of it as poor-rate."

Charting the Way – Map No. 6: Exercises to Deepen Learning
(Acts of Worship)

Title:
Discuss the meaning and purpose of acts of worship.

Word Length:
Between 500 and 1000 words.

Criteria:
You may find the following criteria useful in addressing the question:

1. Relationship to the source of creation.
2. Purification.
3. Increased awareness.
4. Benefits to the self.
5. Benefits for the community.
6. You may use illustrations from your own and others' experience if you wish.

Charting the Way – Map No. 6: Multiple Choice Quiz
(Acts of Worship)

*The purpose of the quiz is for you to test your own understanding of this map. Choose the **BEST** answer A, B, C, or D:*

Questions:

Q 1: Every act is in some way an act of worship because
  A. We all depend on the Creator
  B. Everyone follows his own desires
  C. Every act is based on some kind of love
  D. Action speaks louder than words

Q 2: The main purpose of acts of worship is
  A. To ask for God's forgiveness
  B. To express love for God
  C. To raise one's awareness and level of consciousness
  D. To express one's helplessness

Q 3: The main outer effect of correct worship is that
  A. The worshiper will receive many rewards
  B. The worshiper will act correctly
  C. The worshiper will live happily
  D. The worshiper will be a 'perfect human being'

Q 4: Which of these are inner meanings of *salat*? (choose all that apply)
  A. A change in one's intention and mental attitude
  B. Acceptance of the present moment
  C. Preparation by washing one's face and limbs
  D. Sealing one's mind and heart from the world
  E. Repeating the words of the prayer correctly
  F. Resonating with the attributes of the Divine
  G. Seeing only the One original light

Q 5: The benefits of community worship are (choose all that apply)
  A. Strengthening the community
  B. Companionship
  C. Submitting to the Imam
  D. Forming a habit
  E. Mirroring and witnessing each other
  F. Defending the community
  G. Enhancing personal benefits

Answers:
1: C.
2: C.
3: B.
4: A., B., D., F., G.
5: A., B., E., G.

CHARTING THE WAY – MAP NO. 7: Relationships and Transactions

This map corresponds to Lesson SEVEN of ASK Course TWO. The power of correct intention and the importance of our relationship with our original source are discussed in this map.

Charting the Way: Map No. 7 – Contents

- Learning Objectives
- Overview
- Charting the Way – Map No. 7: Relationships and Transactions
    * Early Relationships
    * Sustainable Relationships
    * Changes
- Reflection 1
- Reflection 2
- Foundations – Charting the Way – Map No. 7: Relationships and Transactions
    * Qur'anic Revealed Knowledge – Relationships and Transactions
    * Relevant Prophetic Teachings – Relationships and Transactions
- Exercises / Multiple Choice Quiz

Learning Objectives

From this map, you will gain an understanding of:

1. Transformation only occurs when actions and intentions are unified.
2. A good relationship is what leads to stability and balance and that is what every sentient being in creation seeks.
3. The foundation of all sound relationships is our relationship with the ever-present Source of all existence.
4. Growth in plants, animals, and human beings takes place in stages because of relationships established at different phases in each of their life spans.

Overview

From the very beginning of creation everything that has come into existence within the confines of time and space is based on a Divine pattern. This pattern has been the governing principle behind millions of years of change and evolution in our world. At the beginning there was only oneness, and duality or differentiation subsequently evolved from this oneness. Man was endowed with a consciousness by which he was able to relate to other aspects of creation. The way man perceives through this consciousness becomes a 'reality' for him in time and space. Therefore, everything in existence obviously relates to aspects that are close to man in time and space while also relating in an absolute way to the original Source of all creation.

This map aims to provide a broad overview of the relationships found within the sanctuary of the *dīn* from a *tawhīdi* or unitary point of view.

In order to fully live your *dīn* in all its aspects you have to enter into it with conscious intent, discipline and diligence. The teachings of Islam provide a considerable balance in conveying revealed knowledge and the absolute truth as well as the checklist of do's and don'ts enshrined in the laws and codes of the *shar'iah*. Access to the full potential of the former largely depends on adhering to the latter.

The teachings not only encourage you to purify your intentions and to have compassion but they also tell you in great detail how to do this. Your refinement and spiritual evolvement are not left as a mere aspiration but is translated into practicable action. Islam gives us a broadly prescriptive way of establishing all kinds of wholesome relationships and transactions in our lives.

Charting the Way – Map No. 7: Relationships and Transactions

Transformation occurs when actions and intentions are unified. Therefore, no matter how noble our intentions for obtaining knowledge or spiritual insights may be, unless they are backed up by the right actions such acquisition of knowledge and attainment of spirituality will not happen.

Everything in existence relates to movement and change, which together form the basis of all relationships. All energies and matter interchange and exchange but only their format and structure appear different–essentially, they are based on a singularity. Everything in the cosmos is also confined to time and space and connected with everything else in subtle and obvious ways.

We are therefore cautioned in the Qur'an and by the Prophet Muhammad that the believers are like parts of the body in relation to each other in matters of kindness, love and affection. When one part of the body is afflicted, the entire body feels it. The believer is a brother to another believer. We are enjoined to foster good relations amongst family and kin and to be compassionate to the needy and orphans. Our spouses and children are to be treated with kindness. All of these recommendations aim to increase our growth and evolvement at a profound level. They are set to occur in this earthly arena, which by its very nature enhances our connectedness with others around us. But significantly our seemingly mundane interactions draw us more securely into *tawhīd*.

The prophetic teachings caution us not to ignore wrong actions that may appear remote from us as they may also afflict us. The Muslim is described as one who is concerned for the poor people in the town to such an extent that he cannot sleep with a full stomach if he knows that others are hungry. This aspect of concern for other people and for all creation forms the bedrock of prophetic teachings.

Early Relationships

Human relationships begin in the womb and start evolving to higher consciousness when the first major change of environment occurs, i.e., when the constricted space of the womb is replaced by the open space of the world outside. Every expansion of the living space is followed by a corresponding increase in the quantity and quality of relationships and by a growth in consciousness. Each expansion in consciousness is also accompanied by the recognition of the limitations of the environment and the relationships pertaining to it until, in the process, the human being ends up realizing that all relationships are reflections and modifications of the relationship between the self and the soul and the Lord of creation. The main business of growth is to move in consciousness from the immediate and material to the subtle and highest consciousness that permeates all.

Exercise One – Actions and Intentions

I submit to the truth that my only connection with Truth (haqq) is in the now.

Recall:

1. A time when you acted upon your intention.
2. A time when you made an intention but did not act.
3. A time when you acted without conscious intention.

In each case, how did you feel afterwards?

Sustainable Relationships

Sometimes this highest consciousness is referred to as 'God consciousness' or *dhikr* (awareness of our origins, remembrance of Allah), which often begins for the seeker as the invocation of the name, or names, of Allah. The practice of invocation opens the heart of the seeker to Divine love. Every relationship is motivated by this love but it usually manifests in the form of a specific need, desire, person or object that may change over time. What we need to remember is that the self will always be dependent and seek to content itself with transient relationships or the objects of its desire until it yields to the soul, which is the real source of its contentment.

Every movement in existence implies that there is or has been a relationship of some sort. In human relationships we consider it good if a relationship leads to a longer period of stability and balance in our lives, for that is what everything in creation seeks. The soul is always stable and the self ardently desires such stability. A relationship is considered 'good' by the self if it helps to enhance such a state. For example, a loving friend makes you feel better because the ego is less disturbed and therefore you feel more tranquil and content. Someone who is hostile to you brings about conflict and dispersion and this detracts from your state of contentment. The self in its imitation of the soul always seeks *tawhīd* and a gathered state.

The source of all relationships is based on the ever-present Source of all existence. When the heart is evolved and truly connects the soul with the self the person will not be out of kilter when the relationships with created things undergo inevitable change. If your relationship is right with your Creator whose light is in your heart then relationships with all your friends (and enemies) will also be balanced.

Changes

We develop and maintain relationships from childhood to adulthood until we can refer at all times to the Absolute Source within us. The ups and downs of human relationships become insignificant when reflected upon the screen of the absolute truth, which is constant.

The growth of life in plants, animals, and human beings occurs according to changing levels of relationships and it is here that nature and nurture play their key roles. You cannot deny your genetic relationship; equally your link with your environment and your other social relationships are of immense importance.[11]

---

[11] The same is true for non-sentient matter. What we consider lifeless and inert also has its own kind of 'life', which is maintained by another level of *rūh*. Every atom has a *rūh* but the *rūh's* influence is less pronounced. There is nothing in existence without a soul. Allah challenges us to identify any realm of existence that is not encompassed by His presence.

As we progress through life all our senses, our mind and perceptions develop and evolve towards a wider and deeper understanding of relationships. We start life with total reliance on our mother and the earth and we end up with absolute reliance on the Light that encompasses the heavens and earth. Every relationship – irrespective of the level at which we are – indicates a growth upward in consciousness.

The intrinsic nature of the soul is tranquil, content and balanced. Human progress in this life takes place along the route towards contentment and equilibrium and eternal on-going. According to the levels of growth in our mind and consciousness, every relationship is as good as the durability and long-term consistency it provides along the path of harmony, tranquility and well-being. For example, as a child grows its relationship with food changes. This change is healthy only to the extent that the relationship leads to good health, otherwise it is a bad relationship. So, to know how good or inadequate a relationship is, refer it to the relationship with the Absolute.

This is the meaning of the verse: *"What you do not know refer back to Allah or the Prophet"*. We tend to seek the Absolute whilst battling with the relative, and so the more we refer a situation to the Absolute the more likely it is to be correct and good.

Exercise Two – The Source of All Relationships

"The source of all relationships is based on the ever-present Source of all existence; thus, when the heart is evolved and connects the soul with the self the person will not be out of kilter when relationships with creation undergo inevitable change."

Reflection 1

Higher consciousness is only realizable by withdrawal from lower consciousness.

"We develop and maintain relationships from childhood to adulthood until we can refer at all times to the Absolute Source within us. The ups and downs of human relationships become insignificant when reflected upon the screen of the absolute truth, which is constant."

In the womb the child is totally dependent on the mother without any awareness of such reliance. As we grow spiritually during our life on earth, the hope is that we become reliant upon Allah and are conscious that we are reliant on Him. That is why upbringing is so important in the first few years of life so that the child relies on the mother as a mirror and then shifts the foundation of that mirror to other than the mother and eventually to Allah.

We should not deny the manifestations of that reliance on a particular person, but then later we see the unity of all such reliance; the *tawhīd* of reliance at large, how it all connects, miracle upon miracle.

Reflection 2

Higher consciousness is only realizable by withdrawal from lower consciousness.

Allah says:

"O mankind, surely We have created you from a male and female and made you tribes and families that you may know each other. Surely the noblest of you with Allah is most cautiously mindful (of his duty). Surely Allah is Knowing, Aware." (Surah al-Hujurat 49:13)

Human beings are exposed to many innate limiting factors and other behavioral aspects that also have to be learned and adopted. These range from grooming the body to improving personal qualities - and essentially to do with relationships. It is to inculcate these habits into society that thousands of prophets and messengers have been sent. They helped bridge any gaps in the people's understanding of such important relationships and gave human beings the choice of completing their spiritual evolution. This process begins in a social arena, in the need for each other, for exchange and interaction. The foundation of that arena is the family and therefore the complementary relationship between man and woman.

Man's nature generally tends towards being expansive and creative whereas that of most women generally inclines towards the intuitive and nurturing and therefore is more involved in the creational aspect of continuity. The complementary qualities of both are meant to produce a natural harmony and equilibrium in existence, which is what we all seek. A woman seeks the reliability of manly energy while a man seeks the loyalty and availability of her womanly energy. Woman is beauty in the outward and majesty in the inward, and man is majesty in the outward and beauty in the inward; when the two combine you have balance in form and in meaning.

Marriage and family life is a practice towards the ideal of fulfillment. That is why marriage is so highly recommended in Islam, for it allows the individual (man or woman) to rise to a higher complementary inner state of completion. Starting with the outer physical – the carnal even – and moving towards balancing subtler needs and energies, marriage provides an arena for opposites to combine and for contentment and awakening to arise within the individual.

The Prophet Muhammad once said: *"The best of my people is he who shows his family the best of kindness and goodness"*.

The basic purpose of the relationship between man and woman is to assist in bringing about contentment, understanding and a deeper awakening of each individual's inner and higher potential.

One of woman's great influences is the stabilization of what is around her. She is, we say, mother earth. Her nature is to maintain and nourish. She is also like water – giving earth its renewal and will only settle upon a rock bed – not soft earth – thus the need for strong men. A woman is often at her best, generally speaking, when she has a strong and reliable man as a companion. A man is at his best when he is complemented by a gentle and supportive woman. A woman wishes to be held in a man's embrace, to be contained, protected, desired, and depended upon and so to be content.

Marriage is worthwhile if it uplifts the husband and wife and helps in developing each towards his or her higher spiritual potential. The most fortunate among us are those whose passion and devotion for our loved ones has expanded to the point where we can direct that force towards the love of all creation and, ultimately, to the all-encompassing Creator. It is only then that the purpose of life can be attained.

Exercise Three – Human Relationships

Make a chart or list of four of your relationships with others. Note the following:

1. How each relationship is helping/hindering you in moving towards the Absolute Source.
2. How you might work on one to achieve this.

Foundations – Charting the Way – Map No. 7: Relationships and Transactions

- Qur'anic Revealed Knowledge – Relationships and Transactions

- Relevant Prophetic Teachings – Relationships and Transactions

Qur'anic Revealed Knowledge – Relationships and Transactions
Maintaining family ties and the courtesies of social intercourse
Respect for elders, love and attention towards children, containment and co-operation rather than competitiveness are the norm for the Muslim family. In the interaction within and between such family units, timeless and vitalizing qualities such as selflessness, generosity, patience and concern are reinforced.

The education of children
Allah says:
> "And Luqman said to his son, while he admonished him: 'Oh my son! Do not associate aught with Allah; most surely association of others with Allah is a grievous iniquity'. And We have enjoined man in respect of his parents – his mother bears him in weakness, and his weaning takes two years-saying: Be grateful to Me and to both your parents." (Surah *Luqman* 31:13-14)

> "O my son! Keep up the prayer and enjoin the good and forbid the evil, and bear patiently that which befalls you, surely these acts require courage. And do not turn your face away from people in contempt, nor go about in the land exulting overmuch; surely Allah does not love any self-conceited boaster." (Surah *Luqman* 31:17-18)

Maintaining good family relations
Allah says:
> "Those who break the covenant of Allah after its confirmation and cut asunder what Allah has commanded to be joined, and act corruptly in the land; these are the losers." (Surah *al-Baqarah* 2:27)

The courtesy of social relations and greeting in peace
Allah says:
> "And when you are greeted with a greeting, greet it with a better greeting than it or return it." (Surah *al-Nisa* 4:86)

> "And when those who believe in Our communications come to you, say: 'Peace be on you'" (Surah *al-An`am* 6:54)

The courtesies of marriage and what is obligatory for the two spouses
Allah says:
> "And of everything We have created pairs in order that you may be mindful." (Surah *al-Dhariyat* 51:49)

"He it is Who created you from a single being (self) and of the same (kind) did He make his mate." (Surah *al-A`raf* 7:189)

"And one of His signs is that He created mates for you from yourselves that you may find rest in them." (Surah *al-Rum* 30:21)

Relevant Prophetic Teachings – Relationships and Transactions

1. "Maintain the ties of kinship even if it is by giving just a drink of water, the best means of maintaining these ties is to refrain from causing them harm."
2. "If I wished to give a Muslim all the good in this world and the next, I would make his heart humble, his tongue full of remembrance, his body patient in times of trial, and I would give him a believing wife who fills him with delight when he looks at her and protects herself and his wealth when he is away."
3. "It is part of good behavior of the prophets and the truth that when they see each other they are filled with joy, and when they meet, they shake hands. The man who visits for the sake of Allah has a right over the person he visits – namely, that he be treated generously."
4. "It is preferable to me that I help to reconcile two people than to give away two dinars in charity."
5. What is more praiseworthy than *salat*, fasting or *zakat* is to reconcile two people.

Charting the Way – Map No. 7: Exercises to Deepen Learning

(Relationships and Transactions)

Title:
What is deemed to be the ultimate or higher purpose of all relationships?

Word Length:
Between 500 and 1000 words.

Criteria:
You may find the following criteria useful in addressing the question:

1. The basis and source of all relationships.
2. The evolution of the self.
3. Relationships and the growth of consciousness.
4. Characteristics of good relationships.
5. You may use examples from your own or others' experience.

Charting the Way – Map No. 7: Multiple Choice Quiz
(Relationships and Transactions)

*The purpose of the quiz is for you to test your own understanding of this map. Choose the **BEST** answer A, B, C, or D:*

Questions:

Q 1: Balanced and stable human relationships depend primarily upon
　A. Good actions towards fellow human beings
　B. Loving friends and enemies equally
　C. One's relationship with God
　D. One's relationship with God and between one's self and soul

Q 2: A relationship is at its best when
　A. There are no disagreements
　B. It is really unimportant
　C. One loves another person absolutely
　D. It reflects the qualities of the absolute

Q 3: The quality of the relationship between self, heart and soul depends on
　A. The self moving towards the higher qualities of the soul
　B. Always behaving well
　C. Forgetting about the world
　D. The soul being like a father to the self

Q 4: Marriage is highly recommended for men and women in Islam because
　A. It helps people to contain their sexual desires
　B. It gives children proper stability
　C. It helps men and woman to achieve harmony and balance in their lives
　D. It gives women security

Q 5: The marriage relationship is most worthwhile if
　A. It creates good family life
　B. It enables a man and woman to develop their spiritual potential
　C. It helps people avoid loneliness
　D. It improves society

Answers:
1: D.
2: D.
3: A.
4: C.
5: B.

CHARTING THE WAY – MAP NO. 8: Towards Perfection & Enlightenment

This map corresponds to Lesson EIGHT of ASK Course TWO, and teaches us about the power of the present moment as it is only the moment that contains within it divine perfection and the seeker who grasps this is set on the right course to enlightenment.

Charting the Way: Map No. 8 – Contents

- Learning Objectives
- Overview
- Charting the Way – Map No. 8: Towards Perfection & Enlightenment
    * Veiled Perfection
    * Hopes and Expectations
    * Witnessing Perfection
    * Perfection in the Moment
    * *'Astaghfirullah'* – Taking Cover
    * *'Masha'llah'* – By the Will of Allah
    * *'Subhanallah'* – Absolute Perfection at Every Level
    * Unifying Your Will with the Divine Will
    * The Roots of Perfection
- Reflection 1
- Reflection 2
- Foundations – Charting the Way – Map No. 8: Towards Perfection & Enlightenment
    * Qur'anic Revealed Knowledge – Towards Perfection & Enlightenment
    * Relevant Prophetic Teachings – Towards Perfection & Enlightenment
- Exercises / Multiple Choice Quiz

Learning Objectives

From this map, you will gain an understanding of:

1. I – *the self that experiences itself as an independent entity* – am the source of the veil upon the perfect moment.
2. The real capital and gift, the true *rahmah* (mercy) is in the moment. If you are not present in the moment then you have lost it and you are at a loss.
3. If you see the perfection of what has happened in the moment you are likely to see the perfection in what will happen in the next moment.
4. Glorification, as expressed in the phrase '*Subhanallah*', is to be in resonance with all the different streams of Allah's manifestation (as in His attributes and qualities) that apply at a particular moment. Each moment is different but His Perfection remains permanent as the underlying constant.
5. Be appropriate in action and do not see anything other than the Absolute One.
6. The unity of your will with Allah's will is vital. Your success is guaranteed if your will reflects His will.

He who sees perfection at all times and yet is aware and struggling outwardly with temporary imperfections is enlightened.

Overview

The unifying factor underpinning all existence and the different cosmologies in the universe is perfect at every level. The divine Creator is absolutely perfect and has created all that is in existence according to His qualities. The apparent and short-lived imperfections that we may see are only the shadow side of this divine perfection.

To further illustrate this point, let's take the moon. The moon is always as it is but we may see it at times as a full moon (when it fully reflects its source, the sun) and at other times not so. Sometimes it seems to disappear altogether even though we know it is really there. The same applies to our perception of divine perfection.

Whatever happens is the result of thousands of immutable laws and patterns that have brought about a particular manifestation. If we agree that perfection is inherent to every manifestation then our state must have an effect on how we perceive things, and this must determine whether we see the inherent perfection or only that things are 'wrong' or imperfect.

Despite this paradox, the human quest and journey is to do with a deep desire to see perfection in all situations and at all times. But often it is unrecognized that the root of perfection cannot be found in time and space. Allah is not subject to time and space and yet whatever is in existence are aspects of His qualities. He who sees perfection at all times and yet is also aware of apparent imperfections is enlightened. In truth there is only perfection and the truth is revealed in every moment and in every phenomenal manifestation. However, any reality that is subject to a person's or a society's mind-set and expectations is veiled by that mind-set from reality.

Charting the Way – Map No. 8: Towards Perfection & Enlightenment

Veiled Perfection

What usually happens in life is that we have specific projects, some short-lived, such as making a cup of tea, others requiring more time and effort and a longer duration, such as establishing a school. If we are distracted from our project or encounter obstacles along the way we blame something or someone (for example, the carpet if we tripped over it or the contractor for not completing the work on time). We do not see our own role in bringing about the imperfection; our own lack of attentiveness, or attention, or presence of mind, heart, limbs, etc. In other words, we interfere in creating a veil over the inherent perfection by our inattentiveness and lack of skills and knowledge.

It is I, the self that experiences itself as an independent entity. I am the source of the veil upon the perfect moment. At that moment I am a thinker who is concerned with a specific outcome and so I compare this with what has happened to my expected outcome and find incompatibility or discord. Once I stop, however, and am confronted with a mirror that shows me that my own inattentiveness and other factors are at play in not making me see the ever-perfect moment, in its movement or in its stillness, then my individual responsibility begins.

But we get carried away in time and we rush. That is the meaning of the tradition, 'hastiness is from *Shaytan*'[12]. Why do we want to rush? The root of hurrying is again divine, like everything else. However, for Allah, the affair is not about time – it is instantaneous: *kun fa yakun* (Be, and it is)[13]. So, I am mimicking an attribute of Allah when I rush. The point is that I too want to be able to do *kun fa yakun*, but I am a limited creature living within the confines of time and space and I have to accept my limitations. And that is why my mimicking of a divine attribute becomes very inappropriate – it is indeed from *Shaytan*.

---

[12] "*Al ajjalu min as Shaytan*" – a Prophetic tradition.
[13] *Kun fa yakun* "*When He intends a thing, His command is 'Be', and it is*" (Surah *Ya Sin* 36:82).

Exercise One – Imperfections

"So, once I stop, and am confronted with a mirror, which shows me that my inattentiveness and other imperfections are at play for not making me see the ever-perfect moment, in its movement or in its stillness, then responsibility begins."

Every person's imperfections will be different. Consider which are your own major imperfections. What could you do to remove one of them, however briefly?

Hopes and Expectations

But I confuse the two oceans referred to in *Surah al-Rahman*[14]. These are the "ocean of the visible world of time/space and the ocean of the unseen beyond time/space" in that I suddenly want to make it happen in an instant but I cannot. My human limitations constitute the barrier (*barzakh*) between these two oceans. I am subject to time and space and therefore I have to take my time, and because I do not, I then curse the carpet upon which I tripped or whichever other scapegoat I can find. The perfection at every level is there constantly, perpetually, at all times. But I have been imperfect in confusing the limitations to which I am subject. My mental orientation, values or expectations veil perfection from me.

At another level we are also the Adamic beings who are perpetually the project of divine Oneness. And while we engage with our outer project Allah encompasses us through it.[15]

That is the meaning of: *"He who created the seven heavens one above another. You see no incongruity in the creation of the Beneficent. Then look again: do you see any imperfection or deficiency? Again, return your vision (your insight) a second time: your vision will come back to you weary and weak from its futile attempts"* (Surah *al-Mulk* 67:3-4).

Our sight or vision sees a mixture of perfection and illusion but our insight reveals the perfect harmony throughout existence. Under the merciful eye of the Beneficent there is nothing in creation that cannot be placed in its correct, relational position; there is no disjointedness. Everything makes sense provided one develops keen insight and abandons emotional judgment and old mind-sets or expectations. Allah says, *'Look again'* because, though we look often, we fail to see reality.

The Qur'an challenges us to find any fault with creation. At first one's thoughts or ideas are unclear, but the more we reflect the more likely it is that we will begin to perceive the subtle mercy of Allah. Our sight will return to us, unable to find fault. The more we look, the more we will discover the perfection of this most intricate and complex realm, how created things are subject to universal laws of nature and interconnect in the most precise manner, confirming the power, majesty and subtlety of the One behind their manifestation.

Witnessing Perfection

The movement or progression from plain sight to insight can be seen in the development of a child who embarks upon life in unawareness but grows into

---

[14] "He has made the two seas to flow freely and they meet, though between them is a barrier which they cannot pass." (Surah al-Rahman 55:19-20. See Foundations: Divinely Revealed Knowledge, for commentary on this verse.
[15] "*...and Allah surrounds them from behind...*" (Surah *al-Buruj* 85:20).

an awareness of the perfection of His creation. Initially a child has no awareness of his or her actions. In the early years of his or her upbringing, responsible parents take great delight when a child reflects what he/she sees and begins to take into consideration his or her environment. This early seed of momentary awareness grows and develops until it becomes a tree of witnessing the glory and perfection of every realm of existence at all times and spontaneously. This is where distractions stop and self-responsibility and the growth of the witness within the individual is established.

I start this process by consciously trusting that everything is perfect, and that everything that has come about in creation is inherently perfect. But now, as a witness with insight, I see the perfection of the apparent imperfection. I witness the two gardens.[16] One garden is the perfect interconnectedness and causality of the world of relativity and how within its own time and space everything follows a perfect plan and design. This is the garden of witnessing perfection within creation in a dynamic, vibrant way. The other garden relates to the absolute, where there is no change or causality that is subject to time and space. It is pure and absolutely perfect before any manifestation into relative perfection.

Every situation reflects an aspect of perfection. With human expectations and judgment, we tend to miss the intrinsic perfection in creation. In order to witness this primal perfection in every situation we need to strip away personal hopes, fears and desires. Then we will see things as they are. Otherwise, our own views will always color the situation.

Perfection in the Moment

If you see the perfection of what has happened in the moment: that all the elements/factors involved in that situation have brought about a particular outcome – you are likely to see the perfection in what happens in the next moment. Conversely, if you have cursed the moment then you are more likely to curse and be cursed by the next moment. In a sacred tradition Allah says, *"Do not curse time, because time is Me"*. Your access to the ultimate light of lights is in the moment.[17] The real capital, the real *rahmah* (mercy) is in the moment. If you are not present in the moment then you have lost the opportunity the moment brings and you are at a loss. Everything that you had thought or imagined is present right now. If you hold on to your recollection of the past or persist in your projections of the future you are bound to miss the convergence of your reality and the Real in the now. This is why the

---

[16] *"wa liman khafa maqaama rabbihi jannataan"* (And for one who fears standing before his Lord are two gardens – (Surah *al-Rahman* 55:46).
[17] There are two terms for time in Arabic: *dahr* and *waqt;;* the former is the one used in the quoted *hadith qudsi*, and it relates to the course of time and its laws and processes, like ageing, decay etc. whereas *waqt* relates to the moment or any given sequence of moments (e.g. time of *fajr,* etc.); in this sense the Sufi tradition *'the Sufi is the son of the moment'* – *ibnu_l waqt is* applicable.

Noble Prophet sought refuge with Allah from the word 'if' because 'if' is always other than what is now. Allah is ever-present and it is you and I who are 'absent', because of our mind, our concern and worries that we have to deal and engage with.

Exercise Two – Perfection

Reflect on two events in your life which you saw as imperfect and how when you change your awareness you can become aware of Allah's perfection. If you find this difficult, share the experience with another wise person.

'Astaghfirullah' – Taking Cover

As we have discussed above, we do not always see perfection in every situation. The example of the moon at the beginning of this map is instructive in understanding divine perfection. At times the light of truth is so overwhelmingly powerful that it not only overcomes the senses but also makes us acutely aware of the ego-self's shadowy existence. *Astaghfirullah* means I take cover under the higher qualities away from my lower ones. I displace them. Allah's attributes work in opposites: generosity only manifests when there is the quality of meanness present. I recognize my quality of meanness (which is also Allah's gift but not His quality) so I seek cover under His generosity from my meanness.

There are three different layers of cover in the sense of forgiveness: *al Ghafir* is invoked to seek forgiveness for my mistake. I was mean to you and I hope Allah will forgive me because now I have turned to Him for mercy and taken refuge under His umbrella of generosity and I know His light covers my darkness and will guide me towards balance. *al Ghafur* is invoked when I need His forgiveness for my repeated meanness and *al Ghaffar* is called upon when He covers my many other vices and distractions.

'Masha'llah' – By the Will of Allah

In the Qur'anic phrase "Allah does as He pleases" (*masha'llah*), the word 'pleases' signifies what He has willed – Allah's pleasure is His *qudrah* (the power to do as He wills) and His *qudrah* appears according to His perfection. His perfection manifests in infinite patterns and these patterns create networks. So, according to whichever of these patterns and networks your consciousness is attuned is how the outcome manifests. It is like multitudes of nets. Try to visualize the vertical lines of a net, which represent the divine qualities, and these lines also interconnect horizontally, symbolizing divine qualities. It depends on which of these nets you are caught in at any given moment. Then you experience the world according to that net.

The Qur'an says: *"Be appropriate in action and do not see anything other than the Absolute One"*.[18] What is the appropriate action (*'amal salih*) referred to here: nothing other than moving away from *'shirk'*[19]; moving away from assuming that you are the independent doer. So, the more an action shows that you are acting only as a dependent of the Maker of all actions, the more you are in *tasbih* (glorification) of His various qualities. Then you witness the one light behind the many modified lights and shadows. You become the instrument of the One. Then you understand the meaning of the

---

[18] *"F'al yaamala amalan salehan wa la yushriku bi ibaaditihi rabbihi ahada"*. (Surah *al-Khaf* 18:110)
[19] *'shirk'* is associating partners with or seeing other than Allah.

verse: *"So, it was not you who slew them, it was Allah: when you threw (a handful of dust), it was not your act, but Allah's"*.[20] You become like the cat (under the powerful beam of different attributes at different times), except that you are consciously aware of it.

The cat is doing what it is supposed to be doing in terms of its nature; it is worshiping its Creator according to the beam to which it is subject. Human consciousness is higher than that of the cat or any other animal or insect, many of whom have had verses and even chapters named after them in the Qur'an.

Mankind has the potential of being conscious of pure consciousness, or even non-consciousness, without being completely knocked out by the knowledge or experience of this. In other words, you are a pure slate of consciousness before any other consciousness arose, before your upbringing changed you and agitated you, a consciousness without which you would not be alive. The world is based on change, movement and energy, which can only be measured against a pure slate. Our senses are tested and activated in order for us to explore and discover our own mini kingdom – the kingdom of our body and mind, heart and soul. This, in turn, is so that we discover Allah's kingdom. Then whatever role or action we perform we are in unison with it and content with every moment of our destiny.

Masha'llah means that this is as Allah willed and the will of Allah is according to His perfection of infinite varieties of interactive patterns and actions and reactions. We are subject to all of them, the seen and the unseen. We start with the seen and the physical. As we grow in age, and maturity, we begin to be far more fascinated by the unseen. A natural healthy start for a child is to be enjoying the physical senses of play and wonder, otherwise something is clearly awry. That is why many people often seem to re-enter a childhood phase when they are older, because they may have missed out on it when they were young.

Living is about being appropriate, doing the right thing in the right place at the right time. The Prophet Muhammad said that the *mu'min* (true believer) has no regrets, meaning that he could not have done anything different at the time. He was not in a rush and was present. If he is put in the same situation again, he would do the same thing again. It does not mean that he is arrogant; he just could not do otherwise or any better at the time.

Perfection at all times belongs to Allah. Perfection within time belongs to those who refer to Allah at that moment. They are no longer subject to their own emotionalism or their own fixed opinions or mind-set. See yourself, but only as a created manifestation of the one and only Maker of that self. Do not

---

[20] *"wa ma ramaita idh ramaita wa lakinnallaha ramaa, wa liyubliyal mu'mineena minhu balaa an hassana"* (Surah *al-Anfal* 8:17)

deny the self, but more importantly do not deny the Maker who has placed in your heart the eternal light of your soul.

'Subhanallah' – Absolute Perfection at Every Level

Subhanallah means all glorification and perfection belong to Allah. The root word *sabbaha'*, implies everything is in submission to its zone. It is really the testimony that every manifestation gives to the perfection of the Creator in His attributes and acts. *"Everything in existence glorifies Him with praise"* means everything follows its zone of the specific stream of the moment. For example, let us take the bees. When they are returning to the hive, they have tuned in to the angle of the sun so their *tasbih* (glorification) concerns the physical beam of the sun – they are totally in that mode. When they are looking for nectar, they are completely in another mode, which is to do with another sense. This is not the same as sensing the angle of the sun. They may use that in order to navigate but their entire orientation at this stage is different.

Also, when the bees enter the hive and attend to the queen it is another form of prayer or reverence, another mode they enter into or another role they play, and when they fight that is yet another mode. So, they are doing *tasbih* (glorification) at different altars to different attributes of Allah. Different attributes are beamed at the bees according to what is required within that moment and in that place and the bees resonate completely with each attribute.

Ultimately, Allah is one, but here we are talking about different manifestations of His attributes and qualities. Learning which is developing *furqan* (discrimination, discernment) as there are different beams of illumination, each with a different set of characteristics. The cat's protection of its kitten, for example, is under the beam or attribute of *al Hafidh* (The Protector). Even if it is your cat and it loves you it will be aggressive towards you and attack you if she feels you will harm her kittens, because at that moment she is fully resonating The Protector. Then when the cat is feeding its kittens and submits completely to that act she is under the beam of *al Razzaq* (The Provider). The cat is now glorifying *al Razzaq*, in ecstasy of that attribute which passes through her.[21]

So, glorification is to be in resonance with different streams of Allah's manifestations, as in His attributes and qualities, applicable at that moment. Each moment is different.[22] At every moment we exude a certain quality or attribute and the root of all qualities and attributes are ultimately divine. The Divine is loved by us at all times. We can only worship what we love, knowingly or unknowingly. Man has been given consciousness and needs to

---

21 *al Razaaq* (The Provider) and *al Hafidh* (The Protector) are attributes or Names of Allah.
22 *Kullu yawmin huwa fi shaan* (*Every day He is upon an affair.* Surah *al-Rahman* 55:29).

put every instant and situation in relation to the impeccability of Allah's manifestations and to realize that any seeming discrepancy in the otherwise perfectly created realm comes from what the ego-self sees.

Unifying Your Will with the Divine Will

The will of the Creator can be defined as His decrees, which are the natural laws of the universe. Your success is guaranteed if your will reflects His will as you will be in harmony and in unison with all natural laws. Allah's will always prevail and your will only achieves its objectives or aims with His permission. You ought to refer to absolute justice and divine will and do your best. Then you are genuine and authentic. If your will is within the prescribed limits of Allah's patterns and decrees things will work for you through a confluence with the divine will; otherwise, they will not.

Allah's decrees are always in effect: *"Surely the affair is wholly in the hands of Allah"* (Surah *Ale 'Imran* 3:154). But man must bear witness to this reality and act in unison with it.[23]

It is already in our *fitrah* (innate nature) to be generous, merciful etc. All we have to do is *iqraa* (read). But read what? Read the map; follow the different directions; interact with the map's designs until we discover that the map was also within us, in our *fitrah*. 'Read' implies do and be, not just recite by tongue, because the entire creation is based on *tawhīd* (unity); being connected and synchronized. In the supplication *"astaghfirullaha rabbi wa atubu ilaih"* (I seek forgiveness of my Lord and turn to Him), *atubu* is to do with return. *'Tawba'* (repentance) is to return back to the higher quality of light.

How do we know that any quality (such as generosity) is better than the meanness we have either shown or experienced unless Allah has put it in us? It is in our *fitrah* (innately wholesome nature) that we know it is better to be generous. It is in our *fitrah* to forgive others, because all of the negative qualities hurt our heart and we do not like our heart to be hurt. It has all been designed already; we just have to read the map on the screen of existence.

The Roots of Perfection

The roots of perfection in all situations are not found in time and space. The foundation of Allah's laws is beyond time and space. These laws are not subject to change. They are permanent, multi-faceted and multi-layered, but we experience them in time and space through our interactions and by moving along these networks and patterns. The *sunnah* (way) of Allah never changes (Surah *al-Fatir* 35:43). As discussed earlier, I will experience different outcomes according to the stream I am subject to or attuned to.

---

[23] See Foundations 2 for full discussion on this verse.

Making a specific supplication ensures I fall into the right net. This ultimately takes a wise man to the point of realizing that there is no power except Allah.[24] And then comes *tawwakul* (reliance); at which point there is no longer your will any more. You have truly abandoned your will into Allah's will and so will always experience deep contentment. And this is the Ibrahimi *maqaam* (station). *Hasbi an su'aali 'ilmuhu bi-haali* – *"It is enough for me not to ask for He knows my state"*. (The Prophet Abraham gave this reply to the angel Gabriel as he was about to be thrown into fire by his enemies).[25]

He who sees perfection at all times and yet is aware and struggling outwardly with temporary imperfections is enlightened. In this world we have to struggle and move. Every movement has a purpose but often this does not coincide with the divine purpose. Therefore, we will often go through experiences which we do not consider to be perfect. Our plans cannot always be referred to as His blueprint. Allah's creation would not have been complete unless it contained the experience of imperfections. Otherwise, it would not be all encompassing. He has programmed us to dislike these imperfections so that we turn away from these by announcing and affirming *Astaghfirullah*. We also have to experience loss, because loss is dispersion and from dispersion we move back to a gathered state, for Allah is forever gathered (the One).

---

[24] *La hawla wala quwwat illa billa.*

[25] The *Ibrahimi* station referred to is quite exceptional and is very dangerous to mimic. We certainly have to ask. So many people hold back most of their life and end up bitter and full of rancor because they were perhaps imitating their teacher or other peers at a higher station than themselves. This station is an indicator of a direction we must strive towards.

Exercise Three – Aligning your Will with Allah's Will

"And then comes **tawwakul** *(reliance); at which point there is no longer your will any more. You have truly abandoned your will into Allah's will, and thus will always experience deep contentment."*

Discuss with any wise person ways in which you might do this (e.g., using the Names as the map describes).

Reflection 1

Higher consciousness is only realizable by withdrawal from lower consciousness.

"Allah is ever present, but it is you and I who are absent..."

Allah is the light of all lights and His power manifests as supreme or cosmic consciousness. It contains all the qualities and attributes that are beamed at us and we find them attractive and desirable. These beams include energy, ability, knowledge, the capacity to hear, see, feel, communicate, etc. The cosmic consciousness is reflected in us by the soul. Thus, divine presence as far as the individual is concerned is perceptible through the soul. Every created thing has a soul which takes it along a spectrum from the darkness and inertness of matter towards the ultimate light and essence, beyond all descriptions.

There are a number of layers and veils between our soul and ego-self and mind, which modify the divine light and render it into human energy, such as the process of thought and all other personal capabilities that we take for granted. If I am preoccupied and distracted by anger, jealousy, hatred, etc., then I cannot be aware of the divine presence which occupies my soul. God's representative was always there but my attention was elsewhere.

A person who is involved in the pursuit of outer desires and is consumed by anger, jealousy, insecurity, and so on will not have the opportunity to connect self and soul, which is necessary for self awakening. All spiritual and religious paths prescribe reduction or restriction of outer pursuits so that the relationship and referencing of self and mind with heart and soul increases. A clear mind will help you with relationships in this world and a pure heart will enable you to connect personal consciousness with soul consciousness so that you are acting in this world with a heavenly connection. You will identify perfectly with the actor-role you have been assigned in the great divine drama, which is under the total control of the Director.

Reflection 2

Higher consciousness is only realizable by withdrawal from lower consciousness.

"The more an action shows that you are acting only as a dependent of the Maker of all actions the more you witness the one Light behind the many modified lights and shadows."

Since the dawn of Islam, many Muslim scholars and *shaykhs* have written about supplication and have used the Divine Names and attributes as invocations. The Qur'an reveals that all power belongs to Allah and the qualities of majesty, glory and praiseworthiness are His. The truth of unity is that Allah is the source behind every manifestation and meaning of events. Appropriate and transformational worship will lead us to the supreme One Source behind all creation who appears to us in pairs, opposites and countless diversity.

The garden is a wonderful symbol of this. The same water, the same sun and the same air produce countless varieties of flowers and shrubs.

Allah's great Names and Attributes are clearly signposted doors to His effulgence, mercy and generosity. When one is suffering from physical illness, for example, it is quite natural to seek healing, thus calling upon the Healer, *al-Shafi* (Surah *al-Shu'ara* 26:80). When one is confused by different choices and possible conflicting action, one calls upon *al Hadi*, the Guide. Then the door of *al Fattah*, the Opener, is knocked upon when one is confined by and restricted in life's possibilities. The courtyard of *al-Rahman*, the All-Merciful, is the widest and most open to all creation at all times.

Over the past centuries several lists of Divine Names and Attributes have been popularized and circulated among Muslims. Most of these lists have their origin in a prophetic tradition which relates that *"to Allah belong 99 Names and whoever counts them will enter the Garden"*. There are, however, a few variations in the lists of the 99 Divine Names attributed to God by the Prophet Muhammad. Enlightened scholars and commentators emphasize the importance of understanding the Name or the Attribute and the right supplication rather than focusing on the list itself.

From the introduction: *"Calling Allah by His Most Beautiful Names"* by Shaykh Fadhlalla Haeri.

Foundations – Charting the Way – Map No. 8: Towards Perfection & Enlightenment

- Qur'anic Revealed Knowledge – Towards Perfection & Enlightenment

- Relevant Prophetic Teachings – Towards Perfection & Enlightenment

Qur'anic Revealed Knowledge – Towards Perfection & Enlightenment

Allah says:

> *"He has made the two seas to flow freely and they meet, though between them is a barrier which they cannot pass." (Surah* al-Rahman *55:19-20)*

On the earth the two seas consist of the sweet water that comes from the mountains and rivers and the salty water of the oceans and seas. The two do not mix, but they do meet.

Also, the seas may be likened to the two states of wakefulness and sleep, or the two seas of the outer law (*shar'iah*) and inner reality (*haqiqah*), or the two seas of the sensory and meaning. Both the physical and non-physical parts of man's life have their bounds and laws; they interface but do not impinge on each other. The way of *haqiqah* (inner reality) hinges on the loyalty of abandonment, which takes one to the station of the truth of certainty (*haqq al-yaqin*). The way of *shari'ah* (outer revealed law) on the other hand holds one to the five pillars of Islam, so necessary because one's journey is in the tempestuous sea of sensory experience.

How can one deny the bounties of either the inner or outer sea? They will meet as they have met before. At the point of creation, they were one and at the point of death they will merge once again. For the duration of this life there is an invisible barrier, an inter-space, between an apparent duality that does not allow the seas to connect.

In the same way the sun and the moon follow a reckoning. They came from One Divine Source and then were catapulted into space as two. Moving according to a certain, complex pattern, they will eventually come together again. There is an inter-space between them that holds them apart as a man's body appears to be separated from his *rūh*. But the body is physical and the *rūh* is intangible; they cannot mingle. In the case of the sun and moon and the two seas are both physical.

There is the *qalb* (heart), from the root *qalaba* meaning to turn, and there is the *rūh* which is disconnected from the world yet connected to the divine Essence. Unlike the spirit or soul, the heart may be seized by the world when it falls for desires and is tarnished by the world's 'salty sea'. The self is then darkened and the spirit can no longer provide the real nourishment and inner comfort needed. When the heart is purified, the self becomes transparent to the eternal spirit and is no longer destroyed by the storms of the journey in the world.

Everywhere one looks there are the two seas separated by a subtle barrier. The seas of knowledge and ignorance do not mingle. Life and death do not mix. Nothing transgresses the bounds because of the balance (*mizan*). Creation is part of a perfect cosmos, not chaos.

Relevant Prophetic Teachings – Towards Perfection & Enlightenment

During the Battle of Uhud, seeds of doubt were sown in the hearts of the believers by the voice of Shaytan calling them to loot, and later spreading the rumor that the Prophet had been killed. The Muslims did not want to hear the true voice because it challenged them too greatly, so instead they heard the opposite. Many of the *'mu'minin'* (believers) who became weak during the Battle of Uhud said the Prophet had died and the battle was over, therefore there was no longer any reason to stand and fight. Then they sought to appease the enemy.

"Then after sorrow He sent down security upon you, a calm [slumber] coming upon a party of you" (Surah *Ale 'Imran* 3:154). The party referred to here could have been the stronger group of *'mu'minin'*, who had fought with all their strength. It was as though slumber was part of their rejuvenation. It was said that their heads fell on to their chests. These *'mu'minin'*, who were totally committed, were in the middle of the battle when suddenly the events began to turn and they fell into a slumber, while another party, *"whom their own souls had rendered anxious"*, was worrying about themselves. They were the *'mu'minin'* who possessed a low degree of *iman* (faith).

"They entertained about Allah thoughts of ignorance quite unjustly" (Surah *Ale 'Imran* 3:154). That is, they did not understand the meaning of Allah. The Prophet enjoined us to *"reflect upon the creation of Allah and do not reflect upon Allah."* How is it possible to think of Allah? The word for reflect in Arabic is *'tafakkara'*, which implies turning something in one's mind with the objective of comprehending it or exploring its full meaning.

The moment we try to conceptualize Allah we fall into illusion. Rather, we should think of Allah's creation and the intricate, balanced, and perfect laws that govern the creation. We should reflect upon the equal and opposite character of action and reaction, and of the relation of cause and effect. We should think of the beauty and the magnificence of the creation, but we must not reflect abstractly about Allah. He is unlike anything we know or are likely to know and any concept of Him will be incorrect and way off the truth.

They entertained thoughts about Allah that were not true, because they did not know the laws of Allah. They thought that because they were with the Prophet a magical change would take place in their condition. They did not realize that they would have to put forth an effort to achieve unity. This message concerns *tawhīd*. – Allah's creation exists to show us the meaning of oneness and the intricate interweaving of its many facets. Allah seems to be saying that we cannot simply rely on the presence of a Prophet for our development. If we rely too much on him, we will not learn how to strive for ourselves, and all will be lost for us if he is killed. In the Battle of Uhud, however, the brave and courageous Ali (may God be pleased with him) was highly instrumental in saving the Prophet's life. The Qur'an says that those who were weak and ran away did not understand the meaning of Reality. The meaning of Reality is demonstrated to us in manifestation as a field in which we can act. By the use of the intellect, we can come to understand that the man who is not afraid of death is equal to many other men in battle who are afraid. We do understand, however, that doubt will come to the weak, and the strong of heart will always win.

"They conceal within their souls what they would not reveal to you" (Surah *Ale 'Imran* 3:154). The ignorant Muslim claims an event did not occur because Allah did not want it. He bases his claim on the fact that Allah has said *"innal amra kullahu li'llah"* – the affair is wholly in the hands of Allah. Clearly, he cannot say, however, that one thing comes from Allah while another does not. Where does Allah begin and end? Whoever does not have an understanding of *tawhīd* is in a state of *'jahiliyyah'* (ignorance). By his very nature man wants success; therefore, failure implies ignorance in the form of wrong application, wrong timing, cowardice, greed or any one of its myriad forms.

We must not disavow our responsibility saying that we did not know how to act. On the contrary, the whole affair is our responsibility and the fault is entirely ours. Trouble comes from us and mercy comes from Allah. Mercy issues from the laws that are immutable. We must recognize these laws in order to apply them, and to live dynamically within their protection, so that we will come to know the meaning of true abandonment and of the realm beyond time.

"They say: Had we any hand in the affair, we would not have been slain here" (Surah *Ale 'Imran* 3:154). This is the voice of *'nifaq'* (hypocrisy) and *'kufr'* (denial) exclaiming fear of death. Before the battle the *'munafiqun'* (hypocrites) could be heard discouraging the Muslims from *'jihad'*. Today many Muslims say that *'jihad'* is a thing of the past and is not appropriate at this time. A person may easily justify his failure to pursue a path of *'jihad'*. If his *iman* is weak he will hear voices that weaken him further still.

The *'munafiq'* disclaimed his responsibility for desertion by claiming that he saw others wounded and running and thus had the right to flee. He claimed additionally to have no responsibility for the loss incurred, stating that all events come from Allah and He did not want them to win. Yet Allah says that He does not change a people unless they change themselves. Man ignorantly blames Allah for what has befallen him, because he does not know the nature of Reality.

Uhud presented an opportunity for the Muslims to reflect upon their intentions and actions. The one whose intentions are exposed is fortunate, because he can see his *'nafs'* (self) in its true nature and is thereby given the opportunity to progress. For example, if we recognize that *'khiyana'* (deception or betrayal) is a predominant element in our nature, we experience greater awareness of that nature and can more easily overcome it.

"*Say: Had you remained in your houses*" (Surah *Ale 'Imran* 3:154), is a reply to the Jews and others in Medina who told the believers that had they been in their homes, Muslims would not have been killed. The battle of life is upon us "*that Allah might test what was in your breasts*" (Surah *Al e Imran* 3:154). The nature of Allah's love is to reveal what is in our breasts in order to wear out or relieve the sickness in our hearts. In this way, what was covering our hearts and preventing us from seeing *tawhīd* within ourselves is removed, and we are able to act in harmony with what is in our innermost hearts. Allah 'wears off' what is in the breast so that it is rendered free. Thus, we are permitted to return to the source within us.

"*That He might purge what was in your hearts*" (Surah *Ale 'Imran* 3:154), means that what is in our hearts is made clear. The message does not concern gain or loss; it concerns Allah and the way we may come to the truth of the natural laws of Allah inwardly and outwardly, that we might unify our intentions with our actions.

"*And Allah knows what is in the breasts*" (Surah *Ale 'Imran* 3:154). Self-knowledge comes from Allah, having the intimacy of a "*He has made the two seas to flow freely and they meet, though between them is a barrier which they cannot pass.*"[26]

---

[26] Surah *al-Rahman* 55:19-20.

Charting the Way – Map No. 8: Exercises to Deepen Learning

(Towards Perfection & Enlightenment)

Title:
What are the characteristics of an enlightened person? How does a person move towards a station of enlightenment and what could hinder his/her progress?

Word Length:
Between 500 and 1000 words.

Criteria:
You may use the following criteria to help you:

Describe:

1. At least four characteristics of an enlightened person mentioned in this map.
2. Three ways a person can move towards enlightenment.
3. Three factors which could hinder his/her progress.

You may use examples from your own experience or that of others.

Charting the Way – Map No. 8: Multiple Choice Quiz
(Towards Perfection & Enlightenment)

*The purpose of the quiz is for you to test your own understanding of this map. Choose the **BEST** answer A, B, C, or D:*

Questions:

Q 1: What should we understand by 'perfection' in the context of this map?
  A. Everything that happens is good
  B. Everything we regard as bad is our own fault
  C. Everything is perfect because it manifests perfect laws and patterns
  D. Imperfections are an illusion

Q 2: Glorification of Allah means that we
  A. Are always singing His praises
  B. Always resonate with His divine qualities
  C. Are always aware of our faults
  D. Are always thankful

Q 3: Appropriateness means
  A. Behaving righteously
  B. Being pragmatic
  C. Living in the moment
  D. Taking correct action at the right time

Q 4: The quality of meanness is referred to as 'Allah's gift' because
  A. It is a test to suffer from meanness
  B. We need to experience meanness to understand generosity
  C. Allah does not always give us what we want
  D. Human beings are generally mean

Q 5: The main difference between a state (*hāl*) and a station (*maqam*) is that
  A. A state is temporary but a station is constant
  B. A state depends on companionship, but a state does not
  C. A state is when you copy your teacher, but a station is not copied
  D. A state is emotional, but a station is not

Q 6: The most effective use of the Names of Allah is
  A. To repeat them when you are ill
  B. To repeat them as many times as possible
  C. To understand the meaning and use appropriately
  D. To learn them by heart

Answers:
1: C.
2: B.
3: D.
4: B.
5: A.
6: C.

CHARTING THE WAY – MAP NO. 9: Principles and Foundations of Islamic Thought

This map corresponds to Lesson NINE of ASK Course TWO and analyzes the tremendously cohesive influence of Islam and the Prophet Muhammad's exemplary life on disparate communities and nations.

Charting the Way: Map No. 9 – Contents

- Learning Objectives
- Overview
- Charting the Way – Map No. 9: Principles and Foundations of Islamic Thought
    * The Prophetic Model
    * Heaven and Earth
- Reflection 1
- Foundations – Charting the Way – Map No. 9: Principles and Foundations of Islamic Thought
    * Qur'anic Revealed Knowledge – Principles and Foundations of Islamic Thought
    * Relevant Prophetic Teachings – Principles and Foundations of Islamic Thought
- Exercises / Multiple Choice Quiz

CHARTING THE WAY – MAP NO. 9: Principles and Foundations of Islamic Thought

Learning Objectives

In this map you will learn:

1. Why Islam is not a 'new' religion.
2. Why the original prophetic model was not maintained.
3. The true meaning and application of Islamic *shar`iah*.
4. Reasons for the emergence of modern populist movements.

Overview

The advent of the Prophet Muhammad into tribal Arabia during its dark ages and the socio-political environment from which he emerged as a powerful force for positive change is in itself a clear miracle. It was a profound reminder for the people of the region, and subsequently for all humanity, of the true purpose and direction of existence. The relatively short years of his ministry led to a major transformation amongst a people who were tribal and primitive to emerge as a powerful nation with Islam as the cohesive force, rather than being mired in nationalism, tribal allegiances or racial identity.

However, due to the unbridled lower nature of man and with the passage of time the transformational and illuminating aspects of dynamic Islam gave way to a more rigid, ritualistic and theological ideology and leadership based on a centralized ruling power-base. This at times encouraged and justified the setting up of monarchic rule, contrary to the teachings of Islam, and leaders who were often unjust and did not conform at all to the prophetic teachings on leadership. With the advance of time and the natural development of nation-states and centralized governance, the structural and theological aspects of the path took precedence over other facets of revealed knowledge.

For example, during the first few centuries after the Prophet Muhammad, the pursuit of knowledge into the natural and social sciences, including health science and other important aspects of learning vital to civilization, was actively encouraged and allowed to flourish. After this period, however, many of the universities and seats of learning in the lands of Islam ended up teaching, almost exclusively, the outer laws of *shar'iah* giving it considerable priority over other branches of knowledge. There consequently arose sectarian divisions, referred to as 'schools of thought' that were often highly intolerant of each other and keen to curry favor with the leadership in power at the time. It was natural for people to try and excel in Qur'an recitation, for example, and the legalistic sciences, because that was what the rulers recognized, understood, and therefore rewarded.

Thus, earlier on many corrective movements, including the Sufi movement came about, and the emphasis shifted and a dynamic, living Islam was once more in evidence for brief periods in small areas. In our times, although the conduct of many so-called Muslims is far-removed from the pristine revealed knowledge and prescriptions found in the Qur'an and the way of the Prophet Muhammad (in the example of his own life, teachings and humanity), the original path remains clear and available for whoever has the thirst and determination to travel to the Light of such knowledge. (*See Surah* al-Muzzammil *73:19).*

The history of Muslims, like any other people, shows moments of glory as well as ignominy. Five hundred years ago the Muslims were amongst the best of creation on this earth and that state can still come about if the light of Islam and the torch of enlightenment are the true *qiblas* (direction) or foci for Muslims. The Qur'an states *"You (the Muslims) are the best community…"* (Surah *al e 'Imran* 3:110) and the conduct of the earlier generations is a vivid testimony to that. The fact that such people have become rarer with the advance of time does not mean that the enlightenment potential of the Islamic way has in any way waned. It is only an indication that the times have become darker and that man on the whole has changed his orientation from the spiritual-contemplative towards the materialistic self-indulgent.

The Prophet Muhammad has said that there would be no time after him that was not darker than the time which preceded it. The fact however that there are, even in our age, people who have arrived at enlightenment and transformation on this path is evidence that the Source is always accessible and alive.

Charting the Way – Map No. 9: Principles and Foundations of Islamic Thought

The teachings and presence of the Prophet Muhammad are transformational reminders that resonated and still resonate in the hearts and minds of all who are open to his message of truth and mercy. Initially, there was little need for theological debate and proof. The early spread of Islam was spontaneous–the teachings were so clearly addressed to mankind's *fitrah*. The Muhammadi model was the complete model of the Qur'an and the way of Muhammad was essentially a culmination of prophetic teachings and knowledge that had preceded it for a few thousand years. He never claimed that he had come with a new religion but was there to complete, in a way, the work of his predecessors and to clarify the boundaries of personal and social conduct or law.

The Qur'an considers all true prophets and messengers and their followers as *'muslims'* – in submission to the One. So, Islam was not new but reached its pinnacle with the Qur'anic revelation.[27]

Because the cultures around Arabia were already exposed to earlier prophetic teachings, it was fairly natural for them to embrace Islam as a continuation or renewal of what they were already used to.[28] Many of the priests and seers had predicted the advent of Muhammad, for example, from references in the Bible where Jesus spoke of another Comforter (*Paraclete*, in Greek) who will come after Jesus, sent by God (*John 14:16*) and then again among the Unitarians of North Africa. The new revival was a natural consequence of what they already knew.[29] In this sense, the Prophet Muhammad's message was far more incongruous for the tribal Arabs than it may have been for the religious cultures established at the time. (This is not to imply, of course, that some clans and tribes amongst the Jews and Christians were not openly hostile towards him and allied themselves with his enemies to plot his removal).

As new cultures were absorbed into the fold, some of the original teachings of Islam became diluted and corrupted and this accentuated the need to move towards codifying the religion. This in turn led to a more structured, ritualistic, and theological approach to Islam being promulgated by those at the helm.

---

[27] *"And the believers, men and women, are friends of one another"* (Surah al-Bara'at 9:71)
[28] E.g., Salman Farsi, son of a Zoroastrian priest. He felt that Zoroastrianism would be updated and renewed, and he came looking for the Prophet.
[29] Reflection on the response of the King of Abyssinia at his first meeting of Muslims during their first attempt to make *Hijrah* from Makkah.

Naturally, every tribe came with a set of its own cultural codes and customs, which was evident in the way its members dressed, the way they chose to live, the food they ate, and other aspects of their life. The new wave of Islam had its impact on many of these habits and day-to-day patterns of life and which brought about some homogeneity amongst the disparate tribes. A traveler today will find clear evidence of this impact of Islamic culture and religion all the way from the steppes of China to the Atlantic coast of West Africa. The varying dialects and languages, cultures, nations, tribes, and way of life amongst these wide-ranging Muslim people are all connected through the practice of prayer, fasting, dietary rules, marriage and other social institutions and customs.

Exercise One – Unifying Factors

1. If you are a Muslim, get together with a Muslim from a completely different cultural background and discuss the unifying factors which bring you together. Compare these with anything which divides you.
2. If you are not a Muslim, talk to two Muslims of different cultural backgrounds and ask them to explain the unifying factors which bring them together. Ask them if there is anything that divides them and why this is so.

So, while Islam provided some homogeneity and unity amongst widely varying cultures, the early Muslim leadership also permitted some tribal customs and other linguistic differences to remain. Even the almost overwhelming power of the tribal system of the Arabs was considerably reined in by Islam and the days of ignorance, as the pre-Islamic period was labeled, were superseded by new measures, which laid greater emphasis on ethical conduct, piety, service, and other virtuous qualities. In this way the tribal influence was diffused to some extent.

However, soon after the *Khulafa ar Rashidun*[30] and by the time the Ummayads[31] came to rule and mini monarchies were established, the old practices from the days of ignorance – namely nepotism and elitism, amongst others – returned; only this time it was worse, since it was in the name of Islam.

A caliphate with a strong prophetic profile was replaced by this despotic kind of rule. Therefore, a new wave of nepotism, tribalism and privilege as opposed to preference based on virtuous human qualities took over. This excessive nepotism and the numerous dictatorial rulers gave rise to a major revolt, led also by tribal solidarity (the Abbasids), under the banner of *Ahlul Bayt*[32] Then the Abbasids came to power effectively replacing the Ummayad dynasty (except in Andalusia). During the caliph Mamun's rule, much scholarship and social and creative advancement in knowledge and education took place. [33]

Later, Turkic as well as Persian and other Islamic rulers attempted to combine kingship with their own modified versions of Islamic governance. The original emphasis on ethics and moral conduct and transformational aspects relating to transcendence was however taken up by the Sufis and enlightened teachers, while 'establishment' Islam concentrated on aspects of the science of worship, codifying and compiling prophetic traditions and the *sunnah*.

The Prophetic Model

The prophetic model is an ideal one that can be applied anywhere at any time. The Prophet Muhammad indicated that the teachings and practices which he promoted would not be upheld in society in later times exactly as they were in his time. Islamic ways and leaders cannot be forced upon people. He understood that times change and people's needs change, and Allah has

---

30 This refers to the commonly known first four 'rightly guided' Caliphs after the Prophet (Abu Bakr, Umar, Uthman, Ali).
31 The Ummayad dynasty was established by Muawiya in Damascus, and named after his great grandfather Ummaya, who had a rivalry with Hashim (from whom the Prophet Muhammad descended).
32 The *Ahlul Bayt* were the people of the household of the Prophet, considered purified as described in the Qur'an (Surah *al-Ahzab* 33.33).
33 The Abbasid dynasty came to power about a century and a half after *Hijra*.

given them the opportunity to move with the changing times as long as they do not try to cross the boundaries of His immutable laws.

Heaven and Earth

The Muhammadi revelations came in the wake of hundreds of years of controversies within the Abrahamic religions of Judaism and Christianity. The Qur'an covers two integrated aspects needed for human evolvement on earth. Aspects related to truth, *Haqq*, are immutable, such as Allah is the beginning and the end and everything belongs to Him. The revelations of the Qur'an also deal with the earthly needs of mankind. Divine justice, for example, is absolute but earthly justice has been delegated to the children of Adam to dispense as times and needs dictate. To uphold justice is a principle that cannot ever be changed but appropriate justice in varying circumstances is a matter of human endeavor by which we learn and aspire to divine justice whilst making mistakes and repenting.

Aspects to do with *shari`ah* are based upon true principles but require proper interpretation, therefore the need for *ijtihad* (exerting effort or endeavor in order to derive a ruling from *shari`ah* law) and a certain measure of contextual flexibility. The *shari`ah* laws to govern human beings need to have certain flexibility because no era is similar to another and also individual circumstances vary and situations may change.

The *shari`ah* is like a foundation that allows you to build upon its many rules and regulations, which are changeable with time, in order to construct a strong civic society.

How do we relate changes in our life circumstances to unchanging principles? To illustrate, there are clear injunctions regarding the preparation and eating of food, but the human situation is such that in exceptional cases you are allowed, for example, to eat meat that has not been slaughtered in the prescribed way if it saves your life. Therefore, the issue of what part of *shari`ah* is flexible and what is not remains to this day a major aspect within Muslim discourse.

Ultimately, justice can only prevail when human beings are constantly aware of the innate injustices perpetrated by the lower self. Tolerance, compassion, and love of the enemy as one loves oneself are praiseworthy virtues, which can prevail for the evolved being whose heart is pure and in which the light of the perfect soul shines through. It is not an impossibility but requires taking responsibility for our actions and effort on our part.

In such a case, selflessness and sacrifice become natural and joyful rather than onerous duties undertaken with only reputation in mind. Islam is based on hearing a message and then living it and thereby realizing the connectivity between divinity and humanity. Thus, life on this earth becomes a prelude and a preparation for the perfect Garden in the Hereafter.

The earth is the melting pot of biological evolution, producing the human being who journeys towards his highest potential. His aim is to complete awareness of, and responsibility towards, the ever-present God. Islam is the path that enables human beings to live well on earth with constant reference to the Divine reality and Absolute Perfection. Towards this end, a thorough knowledge of earthly causalities and relationships are essential. This earthly wisdom is cumulative and evolutionary. Sublime wisdom is transpersonal and access to it is through total abandonment of thoughts, ideas and awareness of the outer. When these two wisdoms coincide, we can say that head and heart are in unison and that is the door to the human journey towards higher consciousness.

The Prophet Muhammad was the role model of a complete person – *al insan al kamil*. One of the most important issues for successive Muslim communities and nations as well as individuals is the spiritual credentials of the earthly leader or governor and, in the case of the individual, the teacher. If he is not complete in his wisdom then he must look up to those who are enlightened.

In Islam's history, most of the dynasties that ruled Muslims did not pursue this policy of taking counsel with those who were attuned to higher consciousness. Therefore, the transformational aspect of our *dīn* was restricted mostly to the Sufis or seekers of higher truth rather than the generality of Muslims. That is also why Islamic civic society and the participation of the public in its governance are not yet evolved in full.

What distinguishes the issue of leadership in Muslim communities is the confusion over the qualities of the leader. Because Muslims love and revere the Prophet Muhammad so much, this is often exploited and abused by worldly leaders with religious pretensions to keep the people subservient and under their control so they may unscrupulously push through their own vested interests.

Exercise Two – Dynamic Evolution of *Shari`ah*

"Shari`ah is like a foundation that allows you to build upon its many rules and regulations, which are changeable with time, in order to build a strong civic society."

Discuss with any wise person one or two aspects of *Shari`ah* with which you are familiar.

1. What are their basic principles and meanings?
2. What is their most rigid interpretation and where is this actually practiced?
3. What is their more flexible interpretation and where is this practiced?
4. 4. How are these interpretations connected to justice and injustice?

Reflection 1

Higher consciousness is only realizable by withdrawal from lower consciousness.

"Due to the lower nature of man and with the passage of time the transformational and illuminating aspects of the path of Islam gave way to the more structured ritualistic and theological power base."

The political, social, economic and leadership base of the Muslims did not evolve over centuries, as it did in the West. Countries with Islamic communities were swept up over a brief and intense period of great upheaval during which the rest of the world's economy and socio-political make-up changed radically, resulting in a major gap in the Muslim way of life and the rise of elements of Western secularism in many Muslim countries.

One of the consequences of this was the narrowing of learning in Islamic educational institutions. Although Islam encourages all aspects of investigation, including science and technology, the Muslim *madrassah* did not evolve to encompass this growing body of knowledge. Instead, emphasis on personal conduct and piety and Qur'anic recitation filled up the lives of the believers. While this too has its merits it has led to a great imbalance in the body politic of Muslim communities all over the world.

The Qur'an declares that he who is blind in this world will be blind in the next. The Prophet Muhammad prayed to God to show him things as they are. To see – not through one's conditioning or self-concerns that skews our perception -- but to see what is, just as it is. No person in the world today can ignore what is going on anywhere else. Heavenly unity is beginning to show clearly on earth and similarly in mankind. One earth, one humanity, one Essence, seen and unseen.

Exercise Three – Leadership (also refer back to Map 4)

"What distinguishes Muslim history, from most others, is the issue of leadership and the qualities of the leader, which are a reflection of the love the Muslims have for the Prophet. However, that love often becomes abused by worldly rulers with religious pretenses."

Refer back to ideas about Prophetic leadership in Map 4. How can a political leader be a good one if he/she is not a Prophet or Imam?

Foundations – Charting the Way – Map No. 9: Principles and Foundations of Islamic Thought

- Qur'anic Revealed Knowledge – Principles and Foundations of Islamic Thought

- Relevant Prophetic Teachings – Principles and Foundations of Islamic Thought

Qur'anic Revealed Knowledge – Principles and Foundations of Islamic Thought

Allah says:

> *"Do not argue with the People of the Book unless it is in the kindest way, except with those among them who do wrong. Say: We believe in that which has been revealed to us and revealed to you. Our God and your God is One, and we submit to Him."* (Surah *al-`Ankabut* 29:46)

> *"O you who believe, if any of you turn away from Allah's way, He will bring forth a people whom He loves and who love Him, humble to the believers, vigorous and strong against whatever contravenes belief, who strive in the way of Allah and so do not fear any blame..."* (Surah *al-Ma`idah* 5:54)

Relevant Prophetic Teachings – Principles and Foundations of Islamic Thought

1. "You must enjoin what is good and forbid what is evil – otherwise the worst of men will be placed over you, and the best of you will call out but no-one will answer." – Caliph Ali
2. "Truly the thing I most fear for my *ummah* (community) is illusory desire and excessive expectation, for desire bars one from the truth & expectation makes one forget the next world. This world is receding and the next world is approaching, and each of them has sons. If you are able to be among the sons of the next world…. Then be of them, for surely today you are in the abode of action which is not accounted for, and tomorrow you will be in the abode of account and not action." – Prophet Muhammad

Charting the Way – Map No. 9: Exercises to Deepen Learning

(Principles and Foundations of Islamic Thought)

Title:
What led to the success of the Prophetic teachings and what were the main reasons for decline of the Muslims later on? What do Muslims need to do to reverse this decline?

Word Length:
Between 500 and 1000 words.

Criteria:
You may use the following criteria to help you:

1. Discuss at least three reasons for the success of the Prophetic teachings.
2. Discuss at least three reasons for the decline of the Muslims.
3. Explain two ways Muslims could reverse this decline.
4. You may give examples from your own knowledge and experience.

Charting the Way – Map No. 9: Multiple Choice Quiz
(Principles and Foundations of Islamic Thought)

*The purpose of the quiz is for you to test your own understanding of this map. Choose the **BEST** answer A, B, C, or D:*

Questions:

Q 1: Islam is not considered a 'new' religion because
   A. It has no originality
   B. The Prophet's message included the messages of all previous prophets
   C. The Prophet was only a reformer
   D. It has no new laws

Q 2: Islam as a whole did not maintain the original Prophetic model because
   A. Leaders reverted to despotic and rigid behavior
   B. It was not suitable for the society of the time
   C. Enlightened leaders did not come forward
   D. Western societies overtook Islamic societies

Q 3: A true understanding & application of Islamic *Shar`iah* means that
   A. It can never be changed
   B. Only the leader can change it
   C. It consists of underlying principles, which can be adapted to circumstances
   D. It only applied in the Prophet's day

Q 4: Modern populist Islamic movements are emerging mainly because
   A. They have been suffering from western domination
   B. They are uneducated
   C. They are suffering economic problems
   D. There has been a failure of proper leadership in most Muslim countries

Answers:
   1: B.
   2: A.
   3: C.
   4: D.

CHARTING THE WAY – MAP NO. 10: Culture and Civilization of Muslims

This map corresponds to Lesson TEN of ASK Course TWO and provides a further analysis of the cultural aspects of Islam and how the authentic prophetic teachings and cultural influences have mingled to positive and ill effect.

Charting the Way: Map No. 10 – Contents

- Learning Objectives
- Overview
- Charting the Way – Map No. 10: Culture and Civilization of Muslims
    * Islam: A Filter of Cultures
    * A Bridge of Consciousness
    * Unifying Force
    * Living Islam
    * Mini-Kingdoms
    * Power in Numbers
    * Lessons from History
    * Rejuvenation and Decay
    * Healthy Cultures
- Reflection 1
- Reflection 2
- Foundations – Charting the Way – Map No. 10: Culture and Civilization of Muslims
    * Qur'anic Revealed Knowledge – Culture and Civilization of Muslims
    * Relevant Prophetic Teachings – Culture and Civilization of Muslims
- Exercises / Multiple Choice Quiz

Learning Objectives

In this map you'll learn:

1. The meaning of culture.
2. The purpose of outer diversity.
3. The factors which contribute to cultural cohesion and eternal ongoing.
4. The unifying qualities of Islamic culture.

Overview

The faith of Islam is founded on the belief that there is One compassionate and all-encompassing God and that the purpose of His creation is to know Him through His great qualities and attributes. With this as the cornerstone of belief, a Muslim's personal and social behavior is only valid and sustainable if the intention is to travel towards and arrive at the door of the Divine. Man's primary and most urgent undertaking is to gain knowledge of Allah and His ways and attributes and to reap the rewards that this transformative knowledge brings. Every other human pursuit is secondary. This applies equally to individuals and to societies.

When different races, tribes and nations influenced by Islam's teachings absorb the *dīn* in its pristine form and apply its codes and laws correctly we find that they first identify themselves as Muslims before acknowledging their status as nations, societies or races. Equally, when Islam is not deeply rooted in the people then national, cultural, and other group identities take precedence over their faith, to the detriment of such societies and individuals.

Essentially, Islam is a path of transformation from being an individual with a personal identity and biography to awakening and realizing the eternal light of the soul within the heart. The transformation from the needs of survival to the delights of arrival will enable the enlightened Muslim to live anywhere and at any time in the world.

Charting the Way – Map No. 10: Culture and Civilization of Muslims

Like all people who rely on religion as the most important binding force for cohesion and solidarity in their lives, Muslims are held together by their faith and the application of the Qur'an and prophetic model on an inner and outer level of existence. We find this thread binding people even though they can be as diverse a nation as the mountain Berbers living near the Atlantic coast of North Africa or the warrior tribes many thousands of miles away in China with completely different languages, social settings and habits and customs. The tapestry of the Muslim people across the planet is the greatest symbol of how diversity reveals its beauty when it is based on unity.

Outer diversity reflects inner unity and these concepts complement each other. Different colors mingle with each other and unify in pure Light. If it were not for these different colors, we would never know their origin is pure Light. So, all differentiated aspects of existence are indicators of something more unified. A rock made from calcium differs from a rock that is comprised of predominantly iron and yet at a basic level they both contain atoms and molecules of the same sort. These molecules and atoms are essentially energies in transit and somewhere along the line they merge into one. So, diversity is an indicator and manifestation of unity.

Islam: A Filter of Cultures

The same applies to human cultures. Cultures often arise as a result of a synthesis of habits and traditions. These habits and traditions are usually determined by the external environment (the geography, climate and so on) and the history and inherited customs and rituals of a particular group of people. These factors also shape the group's collective consciousness.

Indeed, we find that one culture shares much with another when it comes to wanting security, for example, or well-being, power, status, and in many cases, the very means to survive. It is only on superficial levels that cultures seem different; for example, as climate determines this in a major way, in the choice of clothing. Food is another example of differences amongst people – some people prefer to eat yak meat as opposed to vegetables.

Islam cuts through these superficial differences because it provides a way of seeing the One Essence unifying everything.

The Bridge of Consciousness

Islam provides us with the constancy which allows us to re-establish our feet on the path. Within the safe boundaries of its teachings our sights are set on the One but our feet are firmly planted on the ground. The 'mind' is limited and cannot perceive higher levels of consciousness. However, the mind 'tethers' us to earthly things and prevents us from being totally unworldly.

As a human being I form a bridge between the two worlds of the seen and the unseen: I am sensible but I also want to be 'mindless' so that I may reach a new level of consciousness without losing my sanity. No matter how good it may be, one can never be satisfied with only a particular level of consciousness. That is why many people use drugs or mind-altering substances; in order to reach different states and levels of consciousness, or at least transcend worldly consciousness.

Each person is originally a light, our true identity, which is only revealed in stages. The light within us is the energy pulse that makes us unique. Then it mixes with the genetic blueprint in the womb and emerges as a specific identity. Multiple and specific identities are all contained in the One Essence. So, we are one in essence, but very diverse in appearance and culture.

There should be no sense of superiority amongst individuals. We tend, however, to lapse into comparing and evaluating at specific moments when we view each individual as only being the physical representation of his/her essence, as in 'he is shorter than me', 'uglier than me', or 'she is a cripple'. But Islam permeates all physical, mental and spiritual levels and so we need to view people from a different vantage point – within the light of the Divine presence.

The string that holds the beads together is the same even though the beads may differ. There are similarities between a person in China and a person living on the West Coast of Africa, almost 8000 km apart. There are similarities with regard to conduct, respect for visitors, love for the prophetic teachings and trust in the guidance of the Qur'an. Any step towards Allah strengthens unity, for Allah is the source of unity. In this way, the teachings of the Qur'an and the practicing of Islam acts as a filter of cultures in diverse places and amongst different people.

Unifying Force

As Islam spread amongst the nations and tribes of the earth, it often purified the prevailing cultures it encountered from practices that were inhuman, unjust, or had arisen as a result of unnatural habits and conditioning. Such customs that were found to be permissible by Islam were allowed to continue and were even reinforced or improved. There was never only one fixed or rigid 'Islamic culture' anywhere because Islam's dynamism transcends 'culture' in its narrow sense. The culture of any people is based upon sets of values and perceptions, which motivate them to behave in a particular way over a long period of time.

Islam's unifying force, once translated into the arena of human life and therefore its culture, is ultimately neither merely social nor material. The ultimate goal set by Islam is an alignment between the seen, material world and what is unseen and higher.

There are several factors that make Muslim culture distinctive from any others.

It is primarily the *dīn* and ethical and moral codes of Islam – the behavioral patterns, practices, and perceptions of life – that have unified Muslims everywhere and which allow us to talk about an "Islamic way of life" while still making allowances for the many cultures in which these ethics and morals are embedded. Because Muslims believe in the One all-embracing God, and that this life is a preparation for the next, their perception, evaluation, and living of life's experiences are shaped by the extent to which this understanding is allowed to influence their lives and has transformed their outlook.

The attributes that unify individuals, such as trust and knowledge, have the same effect on society at large. Society, in a sense, is looking for the same unifying source. The more a society has in common to truly bind it together the fewer individuals within it quarrel. If we become distracted by the images on the altar, the more we notice differences and therefore more conflicts arise. The more we look towards the One Essence, the more unity we see. We realize that there are no significant differences and that the shape or color of the altar is irrelevant. In another analogy, if we are serious about reaching the city the type and size of the bus that we ride on should not matter to us. Otherwise, we may as well remain at the bus depot and criticize the vehicles without ever getting to the city.[34]

Living Islam

Islamic culture in all its multi-faceted beauty is like the shell containing the luminous pearl of Islam's Divine Light. That light emanates from *tawhīd*. The two aspects – Islamic culture and the essence of Islamic conduct and ethics rooted in divine unity – must not be separated. When they are split apart it tends to lead to Muslims becoming merely "culturalized" Muslims who lose the transformative aspect of Islam. At this point some also tend to become bogged down in hairsplitting arguments about the do's and don'ts of *shari`ah* rituals, which deflects them away from the true teachings. It appears to be easier to argue about rituals and superficial differences than to simply bask in the knowledge of Divine light and unity.

Factors that contribute to the cohesion and solidarity of a people can equally affect that cohesion in a reverse direction under a different circumstance. During peace and prosperity different religions and cultures in

---

[34] People of Allah accept all *madhabs* and the way of the Prophet, and they do not attack other Muslims. It is only because of frustration that one blames others and accuses them of being the cause of a society's backwardness.

one nation can contribute a lot to its welfare, but during hardship and difficulties these differences could have an adverse impact. Often difficulties and hardships will exaggerate differences and people will blame each other and accentuate the differences amongst themselves. However, when major catastrophes hit a nation, they have the potential to serve as catalysts for a new solidarity and enemies will join together because a greater affliction than their normal enmity has overcome them.

Muslims consider every human being as equal in the eyes of Allah and thus during collective worship we consider ourselves to be the same. The Arabic language became a major uniting factor across cultures because it is the language of the Qur'an and invocations within rituals like the *salat* are in Arabic. Muslims learnt the language and the common denominator created by the language generated a basic sense of connection between them.

The connective power that is collectively performed in significant rituals is epitomized by the *Hajj*. The once-yearly pilgrimage brings truly diverse people together placing them under the eyes of Allah on a platform of equality, humbled and dispossessed of any material or social power; the idea being that if you take care of the outer and continue caring for it you will end up taking care of the inner. Outer courtesy will eventually lead to inner courtesy. In the case of the *Hajj* this is even more dramatic because you are supposed to leave your identity behind.

The teachings of Islam bring about a different form of conduct in the household. The messenger of Allah had said: *"The best of my people is he who shows his family perfect kindness and goodness"*. The nuclear way of life today is contradictory to the Islamic way of family life. The nuclear lifestyle brings about isolation and degrades the values that the natural extended family way of life promotes.

Mini-Kingdoms

Cultures, as noted above, are the collective, localized styles of living and the outer manifestation of essential unity. Sound Islamic cultures often reinforce what individuals in a particular society desire. If these desires are based on divine patterns, they reflect the perfections already within all souls; they reflect nothing less than the attributes of Allah.

The individual is the king in his own mini-kingdom. Society is made up of many such kingdoms–some corrupt, others virtuous. Leaders within society can only guide society to the extent that they can guide their ego-self. Society is the macro of the micro. The Qur'an and the prophetic traditions are nothing but the reflectors of the One Essence that is unique and that has no beginning or end. Seeking perfection outwardly is an indication that within our soul lie patterns of perfection; and that is how we know that outer perfection has been attained, albeit for a short time. Otherwise, how can we even seek perfection outwardly? And how do we even know that we have attained it? Each individual is a 'uni'-culture: his/her own culture.

Power in Numbers

The power society and its cultural patterns exert on individuals is greater than the sum total of the individuals. Collective consciousness is far more powerful than individual consciousness. Thus, it is very much harder to change the attitude of a group of people than that of individuals. Culture and collective consciousness wield their own field of power that is more powerful than the field of individual thoughts. Most individuals do not behave in the same way when they are on their own as they do when amongst others. This is a common source of misunderstanding amongst many conquering forces and religious authorities that try to change a people by imposing blanket rules that do not take into account individual quirks and needs.

Lessons from History

Taking an example from the early days of Islam's arrival in Arabia, individuals appeared to change radically in the Prophet Muhammad's presence. Soon after his passing, however, a number of these people reverted to their former tribalism with a vengeance, using Islam as an excuse to reinforce tribal customs and rituals that had no part to play in an Islamic society. The energy field of tribalism had not been weakened, with far-reaching consequences for Muslims even in our age.

In Muslim Andalusia, for example, people were not allowed to be Muslim unless they were affiliated to an Arab tribe and as such someone could be classified as a second or third class citizen, depending on the tribal hierarchy of the time and completely contrary to Islamic teachings. This un-Islamic caste system is one of the many reasons that led to the decadence and corruption within Spanish Muslim society, and particularly amongst its leadership, leading eventually to Muslim rule's ignominious downfall.

Our differences could be wonderful if we viewed and acknowledged them within the paradigm established for us by the One Essence. If all cultures realize that they only exist to recognize the One Essence, there would be no conflict but total unity. Then friendship could replace enmity. All outer differences can become the source of enmity and suspicion. A culture dies if it is not constantly rejuvenated by its overall objective.

Exercise One – Unity and Diversity of Human Cultures

"Cultures are the collective localized styles of living and the outer-manifestation of essential unity. Sound Islamic cultures often reinforce what individuals in a particular human society desire. If these desires are based on divine patterns, they reflect the perfection already within all souls; they reflect nothing less than the attributes of Allah."

Most countries include several ethnic groups and a variety of cultures. Consider one such group in your own country different from your own. First make a list of the things you do not like/relate to about the different culture. Then make another list of the things you like. Consider where your ideas come from; e.g. prejudice, ignorance, fear, interest in something 'exotic', opinion etc. What do you have in common?

If we are not oriented towards the meaning of our life then that life itself becomes harmful to the individual and to society as a whole. So, a culture/society must have the aim of acknowledging the Higher and trusting the Higher. When a certain critical mass is attained within a society, and its habits, customs and rituals take precedence over the inner meanings of witnessing the Divine, society cannot rejuvenate itself as it tends to become fossilized or inflexible. It is no longer amenable to change and dynamism. Its leadership becomes isolated and relies increasingly on tyrannical methods of rule. But if it is constantly aware of its higher purpose the culture is dynamic and vibrant and carries on living and evolving. I am more alive if I am constantly aware of the purpose of my life, its meaning, and of the One Essence guiding the direction my life takes; and that my soul does indeed carry on after the departure from the body.

Rejuvenation and Decay

A culture can live forever or die tomorrow depending on its reference to the Higher Power that assists it in rejuvenating itself within itself, and on the quality of its leadership. If a culture is no longer reinforcing the ultimate foundations of *tawhīd*, it becomes nothing more than quaintly folkloric and thus decays. Culture implies vitality, vibrancy and a dynamism that is alive. The source of all life is Allah. Life emanates from Allah, the ever-Living.

British culture, for instance, has changed dramatically over the past couple of centuries. Yet it continues to prosper because it has tolerance and flexibility based on pragmatism. It has often allowed itself to absorb rejuvenating impacts from other cultures and accepted cultural diversity as part of an overall ethos. Therefore, it has changed radically but has the capability to absorb the impacts from such dramatic changes. As a culture it can be regarded as one of the strongest and most vibrant in the world.

It is not viable for societies or individuals to have a highly developed spiritual side without also using sufficient worldly wisdom in their mundane, worldly affairs. Some Muslims presume they have spiritual wisdom but they end up with neither because they deny the need for worldly pragmatism and know-how. There is a hierarchy in this life in which the physical and worldly prevails over the mental and spiritual. This is an immutable law. It is to do with survival, the most powerful drive we embody.

It does not matter so much how many large mosques you may have built in your lifetime – is the mosque inside your heart built on a firm foundation of *tawhīd*? Allah will not judge us by our actions alone but according to what is in our hearts. Nor by our actions will we ever win; we can never enter the state of the garden by our deeds alone; rather, it is by the condition of our hearts. But good actions performed with due sincerity will help us to stay out of the everlasting fire and be less egotistic and selfish. Building a mosque is far easier than cleaning the heart and so naturally more people do the former and few do the latter. As we discussed above, a culture is also the collective form of a people's value system and that system will change only when the collective attitudes of people change.

Healthy Cultures

If a culture or civilization maintains its reference to the divine purpose of life and Allah's attributes then it naturally maintains its strength and health. A strong culture cares for worldly justice and compassion with constant reference to divine justice and accountability. Living in this world cheerfully whilst preparing for the hereafter is the sincere wayfarer's code by which he or she lives, both individually and collectively.

The overall health of a nation is measured by several yardsticks such as its economic welfare, education, security and safety, as well as its ability to produce individuals with outstanding qualities of character, excelling in the realms of knowledge, ethics, philosophy and spirituality. Essential activities in a society are its industry, arts and crafts, respect for nature and ecology, and cohesion in its families and, most importantly, collectively accepted and respected leadership. All of these factors indicate the wellbeing of a people. When religion is lived it is less talked about, for it is then said to be absorbed in the culture and behavior of society.

Islamic culture by nature is interactive and not static, and its civilizing influence is dynamic and creative with little danger of the vagaries of an artificial 'multiculturalism' being externally imposed, because of the clarity and essentially sound fabric of Islam. During the past centuries we have seen many so-called 'Islamic cultures' come and go but more crucially the *dīn* has remained intact. Had our *dīn* not been split into so many Islamic 'schools of thought' then the rest of the world would surely have embraced Islam in its pure, equitable and pristine form.

Exercise Two – Pragmatism

"There is a hierarchy in which the physical world prevails over the mental and spiritual – it is to do with survival. That is the meaning of Allah will hold you accountable according to your ability, rather than according to what you have done."

Reflect on how this relates to your own survival, e.g., earning your living, taking care of yourself and your family, relating to others in society, being a member of a minority group etc.

Reflection 1

Higher consciousness is only realizable by withdrawal from lower consciousness.

"Our differences could be wonderful if we can find something more wonderful than those differences, which is the One Essence. If all cultures realize that they only exist to recognize that One Essence then there will be no conflict only total unity"

That outer difference becomes acceptable and enjoyable if you take it to its root since at all times the 'twos' of duality co-exist because of the One. Discord is the outermost and most superficial layer of energy; it flows from the deeper root of accord. Accept the outer and move towards the realization of oneness in the inner. All souls essentially are the same forever and yet every cell is different at every moment. Thus, the ever-changing outer is energized by the ever-constant inner. Every movement is different and the root energy of all movements is the still moment. Each sound is different but the silence from which they emerge is always the same.

All glorifies Him but you do not comprehend that glorification. Every entity sings its song according to its limitation of consciousness. The wasp stings you out of love. Love of what? Out of the desperate love for its life! But the egotistic human being merely wants to preserve a self-image with futile consequences. That is perverted worship. A person's outer state/mindset and the society's habits and norms need to be flexible and what is permanent is the inner essence. And if the reverse happens, it is a disaster. That implies outer rigidity and inner emptiness. Outer rigidity may be catastrophic and inner constancy is life.

Reflection 2

Higher consciousness is only realizable by withdrawal from lower consciousness.

"... **culture / society must have the same meaning of acknowledging the Higher, trusting the Higher. A culture cannot rejuvenate itself when it reaches a certain size... it is no longer amenable to change and flexibility... But if it is constantly aware of its higher purpose and accepts this the culture carries on living and evolving.**"

The instinct in man is to carry on and to continue. The same applies to society. The love for the outer continues and tradition is simply a reflection of the passion for what is eternally ongoing and that is Allah's *nūr*(Light) which manifests as souls. When an individual or society is in balance, outer continuity or traditions are more open and subject to change within the prescribed limits, and the inner realization and its timelessness continues on an internal level.

We desire outer security and insurances as an echo of our need for inner security. The evolving spiritual seeker starts looking for the outer and ends up contented with the inner and in between there is the constant struggle to balance the two. The spirit or soul within us manifests a self with a physical dimension and an ego, and when the journey of this life is successful the self recognizes that its real identity is an eternal soul which had only borrowed the body and the ego as a vehicle for this journey.

The eternal Divine light could only be known through its personalized agent which is the human soul which has the power to illumine the self. This dynamic is the most perfect and efficient way to grow in knowledge and enlightenment for human beings.

Exercise Three – Pragmatism

"When an individual or society is in balance, outer continuity or traditions are more open and subject to change within the prescribed limits, and the inner realization and its timelessness continues on an internal level."

Reflect on:

1. The meaning of 'balance'.
2. Examples of outer 'change within the prescribed limits'.
3. How inner realization continues at the same time.

Think particularly of examples in your own life, or what you have witnessed yourself.

Foundations – Charting the Way – Map No. 10: Culture and Civilization of Muslims

- Qur'anic Revealed Knowledge – Culture and Civilization of Muslims

- Relevant Prophetic Teachings – Culture and Civilization of Muslims

Qur'anic Revealed Knowledge – Culture and Civilization of Muslims

Allah says:

> "We have appointed for every nation a rite that they observe, so let them not dispute with you about the matter. Call the people to your Lord, for assuredly you are rightly guided, and if they argue with you say: Allah knows best what you are doing. Allah will judge between you on the Day of Rising regarding your differences." (Surah *al-Hajj* 22:66-69)

> "Nations have passed away and each has what it earned. You as well have what you earn, and you will not be questioned about what they did." (Surah *al-Baqarah* 2:134)

> "You are the best community ever to come forth among mankind. You enjoin right, forbid wrong, and have faith in Allah. If the people of the Book were to have faith, it would be better for them. Some of them are believers, but most of them stray from the right course." (Surah *ale `Imran* 3:10)

Relevant Prophetic Teachings – Culture and Civilization of Muslims

1. "An hour's justice is better than seventy year's worship, rising at night and fasting by day; and a moment of tyranny in governance is worse than sixty years of crime."
2. "Whoever gives of his wealth to support the poor and is just with people of his own accord, is a true believer."

Charting the Way – Map No. 10: Exercises to Deepen Learning

(Culture and Civilization of Muslims)

Title:
What is the relationship between Islam and culture?

Word Length:
Between 500 and 1000 words.

Criteria:
You may find the following criteria useful in addressing the question:

1. A brief definition of 'culture'.
2. The outer and inner teachings of Islam about different cultures.
3. Unifying features of Islamic culture.
4. Weaknesses of modern Islamic culture.
5. You may give examples from your own experience.

Charting the Way – Map No. 10: Multiple Choice Quiz
(Culture and Civilization of Muslims)

The purpose of the quiz is for you to test your own understanding of this map.

For 1 – 3: Choose the BEST answer A, B, C, or D:
For 4: Check all that apply:

Questions:

Q 1: Muslims identify themselves as Muslims first before nations/societies/races because
    A. Islam is against nationalism
    B. They are unified by their beliefs and perceptions
    C. They all speak Arabic
    D. Islam is not racist

Q 2: The main purpose of outer diversity is
    A. To enable human survival on earth
    B. To express different cultural ideas
    C. To enable us to realize inner unity
    D. To show the infinite power of the Creator

Q 3: The strength and ongoingness of a culture depend mainly on
    A. Being aware of its higher purpose
    B. Pragmatism
    C. Good leadership
    D. Its ability to change

Q 4: What are the factors unifying Muslims? (*check all that apply*)
    A. Faith in and application of the Holy Qur'an
    B. The Prophet as a model
    C. Food and clothing
    D. The energy field of tribalism
    E. Building mosques
    F. The Arabic script
    G. Common values and conduct
    H. The Hajj
    I. Different schools of law
    J. Muslim leaders

Answers:
1: B.
2: C.
3: A.
4: A., B., F., G., H.

CHARTING THE WAY – MAP NO. 11: The Individual and Society

This map corresponds to Lesson ELEVEN of ASK Course TWO and looks at how our outer reality reflects our inner and vice versa, and the inseparable connection between individuals and the societies they create. It reiterates the binding force that faith and its rituals provide, which serves to unify the individual and society.

Charting the Way: Map No. 11 – Contents

- Learning Objectives
- Overview
- Charting the Way – Map No. 11: The Individual and Society
    * Reaching Our Potential
    * Outer and Inner
    * To Love Others, Love Yourself
    * Unity of Self and Soul
    * The Effects of Society & Culture Upon an Individual Being
- Reflection 1
- Foundations – Charting the Way – Map No. 11: The Individual and Society
    * Qur'anic Revealed Knowledge – The Individual and Society
    * Relevant Prophetic Teachings – The Individual and Society
- Exercises / Multiple Choice Quiz

CHARTING THE WAY – MAP NO. 11: The Individual and Society

Learning Objectives

In this map you'll learn:

1. How patterns of existence are manifested in the individual human being.
2. The purpose of outer projects.
3. The meaning of the 'mirror'.
4. The effects of society and culture on individuals.
5. Ways the individual can deal with the complexities of society.

Overview

From our human perspective, there cannot be one without two in existence. From the Divine perspective there is only the One Unique God, the Creator, Sustainer, the ever–Lasting in existence. In this map we will show how the microcosm, the individual human being, is a replica of all that there is in creation.

In order to know other aspects of creation, we need to know our self and in order to love others we must love our essential self, which is the soul.

In reality the individual is never separate from other beings. We are all like mirrors to one another, which are in turn influenced by what is reflected on us by other mirrors. A child is much more impressionable than an adult and therefore needs the right kind of companionship to grow spiritually. Once the mirror is fully formed and the individual is centered round his essential being, the soul, then the adverse impacts from society and culture on the individual will diminish. Prior to this state of inner realization, the effect of culture and society, its demands and expectations have immense control upon people.

With our soul to guide us we are able to read any situation we face clearly and objectively without being affected or shaken by it. Thus, if we find ourselves out of place and out of context amongst people our duty is to move on, for Allah says, *Wasn't my earth wide enough?* (Surah *al-Nisa'* 4:97). We continue with this journey until our inner core is so strong that outer discord within society does not overwhelm us.

Charting the Way – Map No. 11: The Individual and Society

You would never be able to understand anything in existence if its blueprint was not already within you. The individual human being is a replica of all that there is in existence. You understand what compassion is because the pattern of compassion is within you. Because the patterns of symmetry, beauty and harmony are within you, you appreciate beauty and harmony. Because the root of agitation and heat is within you, you know what anger is. In this way the reflection of everything you observe on the outside is within you and that is how you recognize it within yourself and outside yourself.

The outer world and all the changes in it mirror what you experience emerging from the recesses of your databank of memories. These reflections also include things that you were unaware of – infinite layers of consciousness and habit/behavioral patterns. These layers of consciousness and patterns are like mines that have within them many seams; each one leading to others that also interconnect. However, they are in themselves distinct from each other – one contains silver, one has gold, one copper, and so on. So, everything that you experience on the outside has its root and meaning within you and that is how you understand your sensory world.

Reaching Our Potential

The combination of all these things makes up your overall potential. The kitten has within her the potential of being the mother, the defender, the fighter, the lover and the one that brings up her kittens to adulthood – their optimum condition. The human being encompasses all that there is to be experienced. That is the meaning of *"Allah taught Adam all of the Names"* (see Surah *al-Baqarah* 2:31) signifying attributes and qualities: within the Adamic consciousness lie all these dynamic patterns.

To reiterate, whatever we experience are the manifestations of what is in one's heart. One cannot remain idle; there is no stopping place. Without the movement we bring to life, that is, without our experiences, thoughts and actions, life would not manifest. One's outer projects, in both their successes and failures, mirror our inner state and show to what extent we have realized our enormous potential. Our strong attachments to outer projects and also the extent to which we are affected by our successes and failures shackle us and prevent us from reaching our highest potential.

Outer and Inner

This does not mean that an inwardly liberated person will never again pursue outer projects. It is the relationship with those projects and the extent to which we are attached to them that potentially blinds us and causes a breakdown in relating correctly to the situation. The outer projects are merely a manifestation of the inner project. If there is a form there has to be a meaning.

There is an identity in the physical world that disperses us, but if we journey towards the inner, we will find it is gathered – that is, an understanding will emerge that we are all the same in essence. We are the same because we are aspiring for the same thing or idea. In the outer sense there is complete difference and separation. But in the inner sense there is no difference and complete oneness. I am an amalgam of this oneness or gathered state and the condition of separation. In a sense I manifest as a result of the two.

All creation was in absolute unity before its manifestation. In time, dispersion began leading to countless diversity. Again, in time, everything will revert back to the same unity. For example, every drop or molecule of water that has left the ocean appears as separate but eventually returns to the ocean. The human soul is also like that; it is the same in every one of us, but covered by its own shadows and peculiarities that make up the specific personal identities resulting from parental genes and the culture (i.e., nature and nurture).

The serious seeker cannot but arrive eventually at the realization that there is complete reconciliation between the infinite light of the soul and the finite patterns in the mind and its value systems. That is the meaning of all of us being the same in the eyes of God; we are closest to Him according to our awareness of His presence in our hearts.

According to the *shari`ah* we ought to be treated equally in this world and so we all stand together in our formal worship, irrespective of rank and position. In fact, no two people standing together in prayer are the same. However, this only relates to the inner and outer aspects of man's personality. The essential project is the equalizing factor and *shari`ah* is, as it were, the safeguard of the essential project on the outer level. It acknowledges and enforces outer equality.

My consciousness is a mixture of an awareness of my oneness and my dispersion. The two come together to form a lens through which I view the world. To understand the state of others I need to replicate their state within me; to allow my mirror to fully reflect theirs.

To be angered, for example, is to identify with someone's fault within you, so in reality you are angered by potentially what lies within you. We are given only a little knowledge at a time because that is the only relevant thing for a particular moment or experience in time. All other moments or experiences thereafter are an extension of that knowledge, which is another extension of the knowledge which came before it. Knowledge is relevant information for that instant which inspires us to act and behave. We try and do this in a way that is most wholesome and fulfilling; that is, which allows the natural healing situation to take root, to redress any imbalance.

Knowledge and action are inseparable; they complement each other: Act upon the knowledge you have and your knowledge will be increased; if you don't, it will be taken from you, that is, you will lose access to reconciliation between the infinite unity and the phenomenal diversity. That is what distinguishes true knowledge from mere information. Knowledge is what you use at that particular moment, which is information brought to life.[35]

---

[35] Action without knowledge, on the other hand, is futile altogether and invariably harmful to some extent, the reason for this being that true knowledge has the dimension of purification to it. One of the main tasks of the Noble Prophet is defined in the Book of Allah as:

1. Pointing out to the people who lacked knowledge of the Signs of Allah.
2. Purifying them, and
3. Teaching them the book and wisdom (Surah *al-Jumu`ah* 62:2).

and this purification of the self clears the way for the above mentioned

Exercise One – The Mirror

"To understand the state of others, I need to replicate their state within me. Let my mirror fully reflect theirs."

Reflect on two aspects of the society you live in – one that you love and one that you dislike. Consider how these could mirror aspects of yourself.

To Love Others, Love Yourself

The foundation of any existence is based on love. Love in the human sense manifests as a result of the dynamics from three streams: attraction, repulsion and awareness of our state. Allah created us all from one soul but that soul is replicated in countless bodies. This is where divine justice lies; we are all given the map to the treasure but it is up to each one of us to find it.

Unity of Self and Soul

Life can only manifest in movement and change, which are aspects of dispersion and separation. We cannot change our environment totally, thus it is more appropriate to change our mindset and read the situation as it is rather than always trying to battle with the outer world, which is not possible. Reading the situation accurately could also mean that we have to move away from a particular environment. The advice to the seeker is to safeguard their state and to purify their heart. If need be, move away, or go on *hijrah* (migration). Migration is the foundation of the path (see Surah *al `Ankabut* 29:26). One has to relate to one's outer environment – that is human nature. However, if we are completely at unity with our soul, then the color and energy of those around us will not afflict us.

All human beings are attracted to every aspect of unification. We enjoy meeting old friends or visiting familiar places from our childhood and eating food that we loved years ago, or anything that reminds us of harmony, balance, stability and unity. The soul in our heart is constantly beaming the frequency of absolute unity, whereas our mind and all of our experiences incline towards dispersion, diversity and discord. Thus, the human being is caught between accord and discord. And like everything else in life, difficulties, constrictions and vices are all there as keys or doors to the original light of the One, and all these shadows are also the agents of that One Power.

My meanness, if seen through a consciousness of my innate desire for generosity, will eventually lead me to generosity. But if I persist in meanness, the inner awareness or desire for generosity will disappear in time and I will be cast totally in the valley of that vice and immersed in despair. My hope is that I can change my conduct, and be more attuned to my soul rather than to my ego-self (see Surah *al-Hijr* 15:56).

Exercise Two – You and the Other

"The soul in your heart is constantly beaming the frequency of absolute unity, whereas your mind and all of your experiences repeat dispersion, diversity and discordance."

The next time you meet or see someone you really disapprove of (e.g., a drunkard, a convicted criminal featured in the newspaper), try to look at that person in a different light. While not condoning his/her behavior, find something higher in that person.

The Effects of Society & Culture Upon an Individual Being

The impact of society and culture upon an individual's behavior is far greater than we imagine (see also Map 10). This is partly because it is not measurable. There is a notion that if individuals behave appropriately society will somehow be strong and wholesome automatically. This is not true because the collective consciousness has its own particular life and field of energy and that is not simply the sum total of individual consciousness. There is a collective memory and behavioral pattern that evolves for a people and nations. This is far more than the sum total of the individual components within that social group.

As time goes by, some of the value systems of society change and modify. The results of this generate far more complex patterns than we can readily analyze. For example, the notion of generosity in a nomadic society causes considerable tension and difficulties once that society changes to being a settlement. In nomadic culture you are expected to be totally generous, accommodating anyone at any time. The desert is vast and inhospitable and one day you yourself might be lost, so you are generous to any passer-by.

Take the same notion of generosity to a village, however, and it is no longer easily applicable. If this value remains with the people, as it often does, then there is potential for conflict. On the one hand you have to be open to entertain any guests but now your life is governed by the dynamics of earning money and the structure of a settled way of life. We inherit values from our past, which are often no longer applicable. This is true with all kinds of societies.

In British society, for example, the notion of fair-play has for centuries been upheld as the basis for social justice. However, when you are an executive in a competitive firm, desiring monopoly without losing out to the competition, how can you apply the concept of fair-play? Sixty years ago, in the West it was considered shameful for a politician to advertise their own qualities but now they will not even be in the running if they do not invest in a good image-consultant or PR firm. Europeans have been, for example, traditionally open to welcoming political refugees and immigrants seeking a better life, but as jobs grow scarcer with a drain on local funding and resources are they not justified to some extent in turning resentful and hostile towards 'outsiders'?

Societies are in transition and must change, and the impact of change on individuals can be quite challenging.

These effects have not been properly understood. This is partly because the field of analysis falls between the no-man's land of psychology, sociology and anthropology. The effects of social culture, collective thought patterns and the popular media are immense upon the individual. Unless we are able to refer to the higher self within us we will be unable to discern the influences that come to us subliminally from society, with all its expectations of us.

Exercise Three – 'Collective Behavior'

"There is a collective memory and behavioral pattern that evolves for a people and nations. This is far more than the sum total of the individual components."

Consider one or two cases where groups or societies behave/react differently from how they would do so as individuals (e.g., football fans, a platoon of soldiers). Have you experienced something like this and how could you reconcile it with striving towards your higher self and soul?

Reflection 1

Higher consciousness is only realizable by withdrawal from lower consciousness.

Social entropy

All laws of physics apply to individuals as well as to groups. We are all subject to the natural laws on this earth. The laws of thermodynamics are easy to trace and understand: energy is neither created nor destroyed but simply transferred, transformed and exchanged from one state to another. As for the second law of physics, which is entropy, every individual proves it within their own lifetime. The closed system begins as perfect and ends up with total disintegration and chaos. A person's physical state grows towards disruption and dispersion, and if one does not realize the ever-Present perfect Source within one then human life is simply a tragedy. As we grow older entropy exerts a greater influence and if it is not balanced by an awakened inner state, one's life is unfulfilled. The same principle applies to society as a whole.

Foundations – Charting the Way – Map No. 11: The Individual and Society

- Qur'anic Revealed Knowledge – The Individual and Society

- Relevant Prophetic Teachings – The Individual and Society

Qur'anic Revealed Knowledge – The Individual and Society

Allah says:

> *"Indeed, we have created man, and we know the silent discourse of his soul, what his own self whispers to him. We are nearer to him than his jugular vein."* (Surah *Qaf* 50:16)

> *"O mankind! Be cautiously aware of your Lord who created you from a single self and created its mate from it, and from them both he spread forth many men and women. Have awareness of Allah in whose name you make demands on one another and also in respect of your families. Allah watches over you continually."* (Surah *al-Nisa'* 4:1)

> *"O my people, fulfill the measure and weight with justice. Do not diminish the value of people's goods and do not act in a wicked, corrupt manner."* (Surah *Hud* 11:85)

Relevant Prophetic Teachings – The Individual and Society

1. "If you want to undertake something, then reflect upon its consequence; if it is correct, then go ahead with it, and if it is wrong, then abandon it."
2. Allah has said: "My anger is greatest towards men who oppress those who are without helpers. Of anyone takes away the wealth of others, Allah will take away his wealth." Sacred Tradition
3. "The people of the earth are treated with mercy as long as they love each other, fulfill the trust placed in them, and carry out their work with sincerity."

Charting the Way – Map No. 11: Exercises to Deepen Learning

(The Individual and Society)

Title:
What is meant by 'the mirror' with regard to the individual's relationship to society? How can the individual live the best possible life within his/her environment?

Word Length:
Between 500 and 1000 words.

Criteria:
You may find the following criteria useful in addressing the question:

1. A brief definition of 'the individual' and 'society'.
2. How the individual is a 'mirror' of his/her society, giving 2 examples.
3. The individual's attitude to other people, self-knowledge & sense of responsibility.
4. The limits of individual action.

Charting the Way – Map No. 11: Multiple Choice Quiz
(The Individual and Society)

*The purpose of the quiz is for you to test your own understanding of this map. Choose the **BEST** answer A, B, C, or D:*

Questions:

Q 1: What enables human beings to recognize different patterns of existence?
- A. Genetic inheritance
- B. Social conditioning
- C. They contain within themselves the roots of these patterns
- D. The unconscious self

Q 2: The purpose of outer projects is
- A. To do good in society
- B. To evolve towards higher inner potential
- C. To discipline the self
- D. To understand diversity

Q 3: The meaning of the 'mirror' means
- A. Loving oneself
- B. What we see/experience reflects our own state
- C. Wherever we look we see Allah's manifestations
- D. Other human beings are the same as ourselves

Q 4: The seeker is sometimes advised to migrate
- A. To live better elsewhere
- B. To escape from danger
- C. To purify himself
- D. To safeguard his inner state

Q 5: The best way for a seeker to cope with the complexities of society is
- A. Always do good
- B. Withdraw from the world
- C. Balance his inner state by keeping a check on his lower self
- D. Follow the laws of thermodynamics

Answers:
   1: C.
   2: B.
   3: B.
   4: D.
   5: C.

CHARTING THE WAY – MAP NO. 12: Remedies and Prescriptions for the Wayfarer

This map corresponds to Lesson TWELVE of ASK Course TWO and aims to provide an overview of the hierarchies of spiritual growth. An understanding of these hierarchies is important for anyone who wants to live in an enlightened way while adhering to the ideal code of conduct bequeathed to us by all prophets and especially the Prophet Muhammad.

Charting the Way: Map No. 12 – Contents

- Learning Objectives
- Overview
- Charting the Way – Map No. 12: Remedies and Prescriptions for the Wayfarer
     * Stages of Spiritual Growth
     * Changes in Attitudes
     * Changes
     * Living One's Life
     * Spiritual Spring Cleaning
     * Finding the Light
     * Yielding to the Soul
     * The Verse of Light
- Reflection 1
- Reflection 2
- Final Note – Advice to the Seeker
- Exercises / Multiple Choice Quiz

CHARTING THE WAY – MAP NO. 12: Remedies and Prescriptions for the Wayfarer

Learning Objectives

From this map, you will gain an understanding of:

1. The main factors influencing spiritual growth.
2. The importance of early relationships.
3. The prime importance of the human will and correct attitude in spiritual growth.
4. How lower tendencies can lead to either worse situations or to virtue.
5. How to neutralize and transcend the limitations of the *nafs*.
6. The importance of remembrance of death.

Overview

Everything the wayfarer does that connects him or her with anyone else – we call it 'relationship' – is simply a manifestation of his or her realization of the Creator and all His attributes. Initially, such relationships seem peculiar to the person (parents, siblings for example); in later life relationships are established or formed with those who bring different benefits (job, money, power, security, etc). Eventually we realize that our relationships have always been entirely with the One, but have simply manifested in these different ways.

A child starts life with only concern for the satisfaction of its immediate material needs and maintaining stability and pleasure. An evolved, mature – one may even say enlightened – person is constantly aware of subtle, inner aspects of his or her existence. No longer childish but retaining a child-like wonder about witnessing the perfection found in every aspect of his interior and exterior world, such a person is unconcerned about transient things such as personal image, worldly status and reputation.

This map aims to provide an overview of the hierarchy of spiritual growth. Understanding how this hierarchy is structured is important for all those who wish to tread the path towards enlightened living while adhering to the correct prescriptions given to us by all the prophets and especially the Prophet Muhammad.

We start our journey by showing obedience to those whom we respect and love and who are ahead of us in knowledge. Our initial duty during this process of learning and seeking knowledge is to fully recognize the natural lower tendencies of the self, neutralize them, and always turn to the higher source within us to guide us. The degree to which we are aware of these lower tendencies determines how 'alive' or 'dead' we are. If we let our vices be the doors to higher virtues and consciously avoid the temptation to follow the promptings of our lower instincts, the higher will always prevail. We must pursue 'spiritual growth' by trying to be responsible for our own shortcomings. If we succeed in doing this, the Cause of all causes will always be there (whether we are conscious of it or not), and will guide us to Him, by Him. Once this process of awareness and accountability is in place and we become more inner reliant, we are also more 'realized' in our knowledge and witnessing of the singular power most worthy of our obedience – the source of our knowledge and highest virtues – God.

The ultimate purpose of spiritual grooming is a displacement of attention away from the lower self towards the reference provided by an enlivened heart, for it is only through a living and healthy heart that we receive the light of guidance. The soul has always been the source of our life, but the 'sick' heart blocks its light.

Charting the Way – Map No. 12: Remedies and Prescriptions for the Wayfarer

Stages of Spiritual Growth

Different interactions within our inner and outer development dictate the stages we go through in our physical and spiritual growth from the womb to the tomb. The following is only one model that delineates these different influences upon our lives. It highlights seven major factors that seem to shape the nature of human beings; factors that influence each one of us.

First Factor – The first factor is our parents and their attitude towards each other at the very moment of our conception: do they both genuinely love each other and are they both eager for the gift of a child?

Second Factor – The second factor is the genetic inheritance our parents give us; our physical and mental strengths and limitations.

Third Factor – The third factor is the state of the mother during the nine months of pregnancy – her physical, mental and spiritual condition as she carries the child in the womb are vital in the development of the identity of the child.

Fourth Factor – Some people tend to focus more on the preparation of someone's departure from this world and less on the preparation of a baby's first encounter with the world. Coming into the world in a cold, clinical place with harsh lighting and strange noises is quite different from being somewhere where prayers and remembrance of God set the scene and the newborn (who is still in a state of major shock) is surrounded by loving caregivers gently handling him or her. And yet this short but intense phase, which is far more important to the child's inner and outer state than is credited, is often not prepared for adequately and carefully enough; the child's whole future may be affected by its first impact with the material world, but we tend to downplay these important aspects. So, the conditions surrounding the very moment of birth constitute the fourth factor.

The mothers who retain a natural and *fitri* (innately wholesome) connection with their bodies, their environment, and their interactions with people, give their baby a better chance to evolve spiritually. If we examine how pervasive the anti-*fitri* way of bringing children into the world has become, we may begin to link it to the decline of cohesive values in communities and societies all around us.

Fifth Factor – The fifth factor is the quality of the child's home environment during the first two years of their lives, and most especially during the first 40 days. Our relationship with our immediate environment and with our mother in particular, is crucial. The noises we hear, the cuddles we are given, the smells we smell, the subtle energies surrounding us and the continued presence of those around us, leave an indelible impression on us for the rest of our lives. In the development of the mind, and subsequently the memory, such early impressions and the values that we internalize as infants will have a greater influence on us than later impressions. It is for this reason that the mother is most careful not to expose the baby to any shocks and major disturbances, or be slow or neglectful in giving the infant her attention.

The trust that a baby develops through the fact that his/her mother will quickly see to all their needs helps to imbibe in the child later in life of trust in the ever- attentive God. How do we know that our Lord cares for us and loves us? Where does that knowledge start? In a subtle way, the psyche, the heart, begins to know that there is care, that we are not alone and forsaken. So many people who have not had the right care in these very early formative years may be severely disadvantaged later in life.

Sixth Factor – The sixth factor is our immediate environment during the later years of our growth – the people we meet, the friends of our parents, all influence us in many important ways. Our education, training, living conditions are important for our development and contribute to our failures or successes and the way we learn and absorb knowledge, both material and subtle. The effect of the culture we live in and its social values play an immense role in shaping our mind and value systems. What others think, and one's relationship to this 'otherness' dictates to a great extent our own behavior. Because one's own mirror (i.e., heart) is not fully developed at this stage, every flash from other mirrors can influences us and may cause much confusion.

Seventh Factor – The seventh factor of influence in our life is personal will and determination, and this factor has much to do with the innate and primal aspects of *himma* (spiritual yearning). With will and *himma*, we can overcome the seemingly insurmountable obstacles we may face during the course of our lives and enable ourselves to attain spiritual awakening. All human handicaps and limitations can fade away in the light of personal submission and acceptance of the will of Allah; with such a resounding spiritual 'yes' all worldly 'no's will disappear. If the heart is overflowing with joy, all worldly trouble will become insignificant.

A person born from unloving parents and who has everything stacked against them in their early years may be surrounded by numerous disadvantages, but if the spark of *himma* is burning he/she can conquer all such shortcomings. This is amongst the secrets of the soul that we are not taught[36]. If we truly want to know, then it does not matter how many obstacles

---

[36] *Yukhrijul hayya minal mayyati – He brings the living from the dead.* Despite all that we can fathom and discern with our mind and intellect, Allah humbles us by showing how the best can come from where we least expect it. The greatest rogue can suddenly be the one to deliver immense kindness, and vice versa.

confront us. All of these obstacles are transitory, and we can still reach bliss. Nature has its own equitable way, but a lot of the equity is unseen, just as the spiritual will is unseen. If one's heart really wants knowledge and wisdom, then the root of that knowledge within one will rise and overcome all obstacles.

Exercise One – Factors Influencing Spiritual Growth

"A person born from unloving parents may be surrounded by numerous disadvantages, but if the spark of spiritual yearning is alive, he can conquer all shortcomings."

Consider the seven stages with regard to your own development. What 'disadvantages' have you experienced? How far have you been able to overcome them through force of will & spiritual yearning?

Changes in Attitudes

Life hinges on change, which is based on the imbalance that constantly exists between the outside world and us. In a Prophetic tradition Allah says, *"Why do My slaves constantly ask Me for ease in this world when I did not create it for that?"* This does not mean that the world was created for discomfort. Rather it means that we are going to be in turmoil until we give in and surrender to the One and only Reality, and realize that the turmoil or chaos has its own order and reason, beyond our mental capacity to understand. Our sight shows us conflict, but our insight shows us how the source of that conflict is in fact one.[37] We must surrender intelligently and with discernment, and not give in to things that are wrong. We have to struggle – life is based on struggle – but not to carry on in futility.

For example, there is little point in constantly trying to pass knowledge of the higher virtues to people who clearly do not want it or are hostile to it. We cannot force such knowledge on to people; they have to desire it and thus awaken to it themselves. It often seems that the biggest gifts in life are pain, anguish and suffering. These are often the spurs that lead most people to seek a way out by looking for the cause of their anguish. These challenges force them to look with profound insight rather than mere sight, and with the depths of their heart rather than with just their mind: it leads to transformation as opposed to mere information, which may or may not be acted upon.[38]

Changes

We all know that certain aspects of our genetic composition are very difficult to alter and are not amenable to change, but we can change our attitude and the way we interact with our various limitations by changing our mind-set. The heart reflects the soul which is constant, but the mind can be changed, for it is linked with the existential, ever-changing realities.[39] If we can be truly in voluntary submission, then supposedly negative traits, such as anger – once it is directed towards injustice or falsehood – will lead to a virtuous outcome and becomes another virtue, courage.

Time and change are inter-connected. Change gives birth to time. Each day is a new day, yet each day is similar to all others. Change is innate, for example in the experience of the seasons. Change is a necessary condition of

---

[37] *Farja'al bassara hal tara min futoor – Your sight will return to you weak and weary*, see Map 8. What appears to your sight will appear differently to your insight.

[38] The world of the seen and the unseen meet in the heart, which is the junction connecting the two. If the junction that connects the bounded with the boundless is functioning well and is firm, then we are centered.

[39] The mind is an inter link between the outer world and your world, therefore it is do with sensory evaluation, and ends up being rational with awareness and higher consciousness. The heart is to do with the unseen, which is eternal. If you have access to it, you will find that it never lies (*ma kadhaba fuad* – the inner heart never lies). But the mind is deceptive, because of all the illusions going on. We must be cognizant of both in their appropriate realm – use our mind and refer to the heart. This is also the meaning of the Prophetic teaching to tether your camel.

time, and we cannot perceive the passage of time without change. All change brings about a certain amount of stress, because we prefer reliability and constancy. Even though we always want change for the better, we also want certainty and stability. As soon as we have a situation under our control, another situation outside our control emerges.

There is a limit to the length of time we have to bring any situation under control. This state drives us to seek the never-changing. It's God's way of making us desperate enough to forsake other things and seek only Him.

Living One's Life

We are essentially spiritual beings, experiencing the worldly reality of decay and our lower animalistic tendencies. As time goes by, however, we find it is our higher nature that gives us full nourishment. Our lower nature can never be satisfied; there is no end to its appetite. But this does not mean that we deny our biological tendencies. We cannot deny them. Rather, we must respond to them and learn to control them in a positive way, and move on. Instead of attacking them, we must sublimate them. Thus, within our soul lies the knowledge of the higher as well as all other emotions and traits in the macrocosm. We cannot ignore any of them – how can we forget something that is part of our whole nature?

Many eastern traditions teach that real wisdom is attained through marriage, child bearing and rearing and living through the normal cycles and rhythms of life, rather than through false or imposed asceticism. The man of submission and unity does not separate from his circumstances, and the situation that he is in has its own checks and balances. It is not artificial, it is real. It, too, is 'spiritual' and it contains everything we need for the next phase of our growth. In its own time the situation will unfold. The best we can do is to be honest, true and sincere to ourselves.

Wayfarers must take everything in their stride and maintain a sense of humor. All of life is humorous in a certain way. The joke is on us to see if we realize that the whole thing does not matter in the long run. Ultimately, we are going to die, and any particular situation that we consider important will not last. So, we must not take it too seriously.[40] We are no sooner born when we begin to die. How can we take our situation seriously? We must, however, take honesty and truth seriously. If we are in true submission, we spontaneously know the true intention of Reality because we have dissolved our will into Its will. The man of submission is the man of unity. Indeed, the path of submission is the path of unity.

This world is one of separation, and we all experience this separation whilst yearning for the unity found in the original gathered state. The Day of

---

[40] We must not mix this up with being irresponsible in our outer affairs. Refer to Foundations in Map 8 on how 'the two oceans' meet, but there is a barrier between them.

Reckoning is a universal return to such a gathered state. Then, we can look back and see the perfection even in that so-called failing; then we can move on. For example, there is outer failure when a stone hits you. But there is perfection in the event in the fact that the stone was obeying the laws of gravity and you happened to be walking in its trajectory at that precise moment. Every moment has its perfection, but it is we who are often looking at imperfection.

The sincere wayfarer does not repeat the same mistake. As wayfarers we will discover that prayer is our source of connection to our selves with the One and only Reality. That means we are no longer connecting our selves to our desires and expectations. If we leave behind lower desires, we will then embrace truly worthy desires and expectations. Whether we like it or not, the truth always prevails and everything else reflects aspects of the truth. Outer manifestations of the truth will portray themselves as the only reality to us but will in fact only be transient phenomena.

We can also say that absolute reality is founded upon one truth that exhibits diverse and constantly changing characteristics. All changes are energized by the source that never ever changes.

Every human being has a profound experience at certain points in their life when they gain access to the joy of knowing for certain that they are not who they thought they were; not a random accident but a purpose-filled part of a whole. This happens when the shadow of the ego disappears for a tantalizing moment. All that happens during such moments is that the rust that has darkened the heart and prevented the *rūh* from shining, has been lifted.

Spiritual Spring Cleaning

That is why there is a lot of deep cleaning to be done as early as possible, until these layers and layers of rust have been removed. Once this is done, merely wiping the heart cleans it, and it becomes easier to do. This is similar to the glass cover of old oil lamps that had to have the soot scraped off to begin with; but once cleaned, they just needed wiping over lightly. We have to wipe our hearts at least five times a day formally by performing *salat*. This is because in prayer we connect with the soul and all souls know each other. The reason we see each other as different is because so many layers of the *nafs* cover the soul and this prevents communication with other souls. The other souls also have their covers, and this leads to countless misunderstandings between individuals, communities and nations.

The advice to the wayfarer is to put him or herself into situations where this rust wears off more often and easily. It happens in circles of *dhikr*[41] where people remind you of your higher virtues, through fasting, giving *zakat*, going

---

[41] *'dhikr'* means remembrance, and usually refers to remembrance of Allah.

for Hajj or *umra*, and undertaking good actions and abstaining from the unfavorable ones. It also occurs after a major shock or near-death experience. When you remember death, you are reminded of what is in your pre-memory. It ought to be borne in mind that memory is only a shadow of its original foundation. The same thing applies to consciousness. There is primal consciousness of the One Reality that the baby is born with. But he has no consciousness of anything else, or even of any definable entity such as 'mother' or 'milk'. But there is consciousness, as there is memory, even in babies.

Allah says in the Qur'an, *"Has there been a time before man [appeared – a time] when he was not yet a thing to be thought of?"* (Surah *al-Insan* 76:1) The answer is both yes and no. Yes, in that man could not be 'thought of' or mentioned before his existence in this creational realm bounded by space and time. There is certainly a time when man could be 'thought of', in the original tableau – in that boundless realm before creation. So, the advice is to go beyond the limitations of your physicality, identity and mental boundaries. The question is how? It is by living the practices, as explained in the maps that constitute this Course, thus transcending, without denying, the material and rational side of us. That is why religions have to have a structure – one cannot treat this matter casually or in jest. Like cars and rockets that take us from A to B, religion, too, needs a structure to guide us along the path to wholesome living.

The purpose of the rocket is to take off into space but it cannot do so without a structure and foundation. The foundation is bound and defined, and the same is true with the *dīn* of Islam. You have to adhere to and build on the foundations, because no matter who you are, it is the foundations that liberate you. You have to adhere to an applicable and usable system of worship that has been revealed. Islam is a blueprint that is usable by anyone at any time and place; there is no need to carry a mosque on your back or any other baggage–cultural or otherwise.

Wherever you go you can disappear from your own narrow identity and find Allah's light shining for you and guiding you. If you live by your heart, you will live forever in your inner mosque.

Finding the Light

If you recognize the light and at the same time admit that you have been in denial but want to sincerely change you are at the threshold of leaving all lies and denial behind. You need to face the lower tendencies courageously and come out on the other side. Vices can be slippery paths to worse situations, or they can be doors to virtue. If the *raqib* (watchful vigilance) within you catches your meanness and then beams the immense generosity of Allah at you, then your state of meanness alters and turns into generosity or, at the very least, becomes a neutral state.

The self is always dark until it acknowledges the supremacy of the soul and submits to this. The mind is also always limited. The soul, however, is always illumined and the heart leads us to the heavens. What constitutes the human framework is a combination of these two binary positions and your state depends on the door on which you knock.

If the seeker of truth reads the situation accurately and honestly then evolution and growth will naturally occur. To be protected from the ever-changing layers of the self, we need to understand the real nature of the lower ego-self and then transcend it forever.

In order to understand the ego-self we need to reflect on Allah's immense, sublime majesty. Where the self is fearful and cowardly; Allah is the source of peace and courage. Where the self is full of hate and envy; Allah is the source of love, magnanimity and generosity. The self is impatient, Allah is ever patient. Passion and lust engulf the ego-self; Allah is the source of pure love and nurturing. Look at the lower tendencies of the self and then visualize Allah's high attributes so that they (the attributes) cover and overcome the ego-self. The self starts off, bare and unconditional, as a block of clay waiting to be molded, yet exhibits false pride and arrogance as it interacts with the world.

Exercise Two – Changing Attitudes

"You need to face the lower tendencies courageously and come out on the other side. Vices can be slippery paths to worse situations or can be doors to virtue."

Reflect on one or two of your lower tendencies. Consider how they could lead to 'worse situations' or how, by changing your attitude, they could be 'doors to virtue'.

Yielding to the Soul

The remedy for any of these vices within the self is to recognize the worst of its type and acknowledge your revulsion of it. You then look at Allah's immense generosity towards you in providing you access to His beautiful names and attributes, and reflect an aspect of these in your being and behavior. Take all things to their absolute and The Absolute (Allah) will cover or more than compensate for them. The ego-self tries to imitate the high attributes just as a commoner pretends to be a king; through a pure heart, the ego-self can learn to allow the *rūh* (soul) to lead and shed the light of truth upon the transient realities experienced by an individual.

This is not, however, to completely denounce the ego-self. A major part of our ability to be alive and function on this earth may be attributed to the ego-self. The ego-self is such that it gives first priority to the body. Your *nafs* drives you and without it you would not survive on the earth, in this world. Without earth there is no existence and we must love and respect the earth as it is a manifestation of divine creativity and mercy. We must denounce '*dunya*'[42], which represents our attachment, love and secret desires for worldly things. We must be watchful of the machinations of our ego and its vanity and not attack our *nafs*, which is part of Allah's perfect design. The *nafs* is another entity; it is not the same as the *rūh*. The *rūh* cannot be fathomed in any way because it is cosmic and beyond our ability to comprehend, whereas the *nafs* is easily discernible.

The *nafs* will experience death and therefore fears it, thus trying to prolong life. The *rūh* is forever and will continue after death, modified by the accumulated experiences and actions of the *nafs*. To remember death is another great remedy with which to deflate the *nafs* and to serve as an antidote to its lower tendencies. In our world, all mention of death or painful experiences is considered undesirable. We choose the outwardly presentable and end up with much inner sickness. We forget that to achieve outer ease we must awaken through inner difficulty. To know eternal life, we must be willing to die in the world of space and time. Society seeks outer security but often ends up insecure inwardly. If we accept the natural gift of never attaining contentment and security in the outer, then we will obviously turn to look for contentment and security in the inner.

He is the Light of lights, which is why He is the only unique truth. Everything else in existence is a duality. If it is not doubled in a material sense then it is doubled in subtle ways in patterns seen and unseen. Nothing in existence can ever happen without it having its opposite effect. The One and only Creator alone remains unaffected. That is why *Wahid al Ahad* cannot be

---

[42] '*dunya*' means worldliness; in the sense of our attachments to the world.

fathomed by us. The Prophet advised us to not discuss Allah but to discuss His attributes, His qualities, His Names and His infinite layers of power and manifestation.

The Verse of Light

There are several verses in the Qur'an that describe the spiritual essence of man and the intimate connection between the human and the divine. The Verse of Light (*Ayat al-Nūr* in *Surat al-Nūr* 24:35), is particularly relevant to our attempts to look at the subtle depths of meaning of life. Numerous references can be found in the religions as to how God created man in His *surat* or *shaakila*, that is, in His likeness or image. One of the ways we may interpret this phrase is that the human being contains within his/her essence all that is admirable or praiseworthy about God. Whatever you praise, admire and love is one of Allah's attributes. The human soul already knew the sacred attributes and qualities of Allah when he arrived on earth. Allah describes this in the Qur'an as '*sibghatul* Allah' – the color of Allah. The foundation upon which creation is based is the divine attributes of love, compassion and generosity.

When the heart resonates with the color energy of compassion, we shall experience unconditional love and mercy. All desirable qualities are there for us to be attuned to them. This implies neutrality at heart and willingness and capacity to resonate with these higher states.

> "*Allah is the Light (*Nūr*) of the heavens and the earth. The parable of His Light is, as it were, that of a niche (*mishkaat*) containing a lamp (*misbah*); the lamp is [enclosed] in glass (*zujaaja*), the glass [shining] like a radiant star: a lamp lit from a blessed tree (*shajaratim mubaarakatin zaytuna*) – an olive tree that is neither of the east nor the west – the oil whereof [is so bright that it] would well nigh give light [of itself] even though fire had not touched it: Light upon light! Allah guides unto His light whom that wills [to be guided]; and [to this end] Allah sets forth parables for people, since Allah [alone] has full knowledge of all things.*" (Surah al-Nūr 24:35)

The example or parable of the Verse of Light may refer to the *mishkaat* (which is defined as a body, a niche, a corner, an alcove) as a metaphor of the human body.

Continuing with the exegesis of *Ayat al Nur*, the niche symbolizes a body, a physical entity whose origin is light but which appears in physical form. From its subtlest origins, it has manifested through many stages and modifications and has ended up as solid matter. This metaphorical niche is the human body. All matter can be imagined as 'frozen' light or energy, for a while.

Misbah or lamp implies the light within which is the *rūh* or spirit or soul. When the *rūh* leaves the body, its source of life or energy has left and thus the body decomposes and returns to its earthly origin.

"Al misbahu fezujaaja" (the lamp is in a glass) – this sacred light is protected by a glass cover.

"Az-zujaaja ka annaha kawkabun durriyya" (the glass itself is like a brightly shining star) and houses the light. This illuminated glass cover refers to the heart; the abode of the soul is the heart.

"Yuqadu min shajaratim mubaarakatin zaytuna la sharqiyyatin wa la gharbiyya" (it is light by oil from a blessed olive tree, neither of the East nor the West) – this soul or energy that gives such incomparable luminosity flows from a tree that is blessed, which is not earthly and belongs neither to the East nor the West. The reference to the East also implies coming to life (the sunrise), and the West implies dying (with the sun setting). The soul is eternal, whereas the body is subject to life and death.

The reference to the unique olive tree and its sacred oil reminds us of the gift of nature of the earthly olive tree which can live for thousands of years in the harshest of conditions, without much care. Yet its flowers and fruits are delicate and delightfully soft. From the seed of the fruit comes the oil which is versatile and has numerous uses. Not very long ago, the measure of a person's wealth was reckoned by the number of vats of olive oil that he possessed.

"Yakaadu zaytuha yudhiu wa law lam tamsas hu nar" (the oil gives light, though fire does not touch it) – this oil, essence or light, is naturally illumined, without fire, a reflection that "Allah is the light of the heavens and earth". This special oil gives off brilliant light without any earthly burning. *Nar* (fire) is an aspect or a branch of *Nūr* (light). The word *nar* relates to the word *nur*, and from *nūr* – light – comes everything else.

The parable is that a human being is essentially alive due to the inner light. In summary, the Verse of Light speaks of: a material body (the niche), which contains a luminous light (the spirit or soul, *rūh*), encased within a protective cover (the heart), that is of itself, luminous.

'Nurun ala nur' (light upon light) – one of the interpretations of this is that if you are seeking consciously a subtler light, then you absorb more of that original light. Allah will guide you by His light.

Since all of creation has emanated from the original divine, pure light, then the more frequently we refer, remember and recall, or supplicate to that light, the more spiritual growth is attained.

Our desire to know and understand and be enlightened implies connecting and unifying with the Light of lights by the mercy of Allah. The myriad manifestations of the light and its shadows can cause distraction and confusion regarding their origin in the Light of lights. The essence of the human being is the sacred light of the soul and as such we have the potential to know what is on earth and in heaven.

Reflection 1

Higher consciousness is only realizable by withdrawal from lower consciousness.

"Make your duty towards avoiding the lower, and the higher will always prevail. Do not demand spiritual growth – be responsible for your own short-comings and the Cause of all causes will always be there, and will guide you to Him by Him."

The following is a very key issue in our teachings. So many people claim "I want Allah", implying that we can somehow have and know the Absolute. The teachings contained in this Course stop us from this absurdity. Rather, we are told to turn away from *Shaytan*, because we cannot talk about wanting the essence of Allah. The Prophet told us not to talk about the essence of Allah, the Absolute, but we fail to translate this into action.

The real meaning of the prophetic counsel is to refrain from making such spiritual claims and engaging in such spiritual fantasies – 'wanting Allah' implies that He can be encompassed by our minds and somehow contained within our narrow conceptualizations of Him. We should instead be looking at our own stupidities, acts of irresponsibility and waywardness. This is what we need to rectify, because the higher has always been there. Claims of seeking the higher are more often an avoidance of responsibility – "I'm seeking the higher, leave me to my hermit's cave." Allah does not need any of our services; it is we who need to bring our egos in line with the expectations of the higher. This is what is missing. Rather than talk about Allah, let us talk about our vanities and vices, and then try to turn them into reflections of Allah's virtues.

If you are truly centered, in the middle of the road (*ummatun wassata* – the people of the middle path), then you will be able to see both extremes. At one end is my *Shaytan*, and at the other end is the overall *Rahman*. If you are at either edge, your vision will be confined to that edge. From the center you see the trivialities and desires of the *nafs* and you do not deny them. Nor do you let them overwhelm you because the light of *Rahman* in you guides you. You should never deny any of the lower tendencies; they are an integral part of your make-up and you are able to recognize them because they are in you. Compassion is knowing and acknowledging all the weaknesses in one, but more than that one's attention is *dhikr* (remembrance) and awareness of all of Allah's qualities and virtues. And *astaghfirullah* is seeking to cover one's weaknesses with Allah's virtues. We have both *Rahman* and *Shaytan* within us, and Shaytan is there to hurt and afflict us so that we turn away from him to *Rahman*. He is actually Allah's agent within us. Shaykh Abul Hassan Shadhili has said we should not curse Shaytan, rather we should consider him as a sort of cloth that Allah has given us to spit on. Without this aspect of *Shaytan* for us to spit on and turn away from, we would not be able to 'turn to' the higher.

In this way *Shaytan* becomes a most positive and useful instrument, a most positive fire to drive us away from all sorts of negativity – fear of provision, fear of reputation, greed, lust, etc.

First, we ought to witness the lower (fear, hatred, meanness, etc.) and realize our dislike of these tendencies. Then we need to reflect upon their opposites (love, generosity, patience, etc.) which we had already experienced in the past. Then we allow the higher attribute/s to cover and overwhelm our little vice/s.

Reflection 2

Higher consciousness is only realizable by withdrawal from lower consciousness.

"**Allah is the Light of the Heavens and the earth. The parable of His light is as if there were a niche and within it a lamp: the lamp is in a glass, the glass as it were a brilliant star, lit from a blessed tree, an olive, neither of the East nor of the West but it is exposed to the sun all day long, whose oil would almost glow forth (of itself), though no fire touched it. Light upon Light! Allah guides to His wills. And Allah sets forth parables for mankind, and Allah is all-Knower of everything."** (*Surah Al-Nur: 24:35*)

The Adamic Blueprint

As noted earlier, the creation of Adam was the culmination of all patterns and every manifestation in existence. There is no possibility for a creation or a permutation not to exist. That is why Allah's creations are countless. The culmination of all of these creations which contain within them the knowledge, or the patterns of all these other creations, is the creation of Adam - the Adamic blueprint, the Adamic soul. He is thus referred to as the *khalifa* (representative), he who is present in the apparent absence of the ultimate master. He is the representative of the true ever-lasting Lord and Master. So, Adam, and all of us human beings, have been given this responsibility of having the potential of knowing the purpose, the direction, and the meaning of all of existence - it lies within us. We can understand how the ant, the mountains, stones and so on gravitate and relate to each other and everything else; how things come and go in existence. So, within us lie the entire cosmic possibilities. Therefore, Adam or man, in a sense, contains within him the original tableaux of everything that has happened, can happen or will happen.

This means that within the Adamic heart lies this facet or entity that is not subject to time and space. God is not subject to time and space. He created time and space as little illusions in which to contain His creation to realize that they have descended from one reality, are sustained by One reality, are returning to one reality, that is, there is only one reality. Every other reality is short-lived and temporal. This reality is the truth; other realities come and go and shift. Thus, the potentiality within the breast of Adam is divine. Therefore, human beings contain within them a divine principle, and that divine principle is the constancy of the soul within them. In their life's experience they go through layer after layer of different levels of consciousness but the soul remains constant.

The child's consciousness is different from the teenager's consciousness, which in turn is different from the adult's consciousness, which is also different from the 'contented heart's' consciousness, and many other different layers, as we have seen. Also, there is a constant inter-mingling of these various layers of consciousness in a web of consciousness. Ultimately there is a hierarchy of consciousness, and this hierarchy relates to ongoing. Thus, if you are conscious of a bird singing and a limb is suddenly injured, then you immediately respond to that consciousness of injury, because that harms you. Therefore, there is a hierarchy. That is why it is said "clean your clothes"[43], then you can clean your heart. You must start with the outer – your conduct, your relationships – and if you continue with this with sincerity and true understanding, your inner will end up being right.

So, everything is a description of the position of Adam in this existence. *Ayat al Nūr* (Surah *al-Nūr* 24:35) gives a full map in a *mithal* (as a parable). *"Allah is the light of the heavens and the earth"*. It means that the foundation of whatever is in the heavens or the earth is light. Its root energy is light. Many of these lights can be said to be conditioned lights. One of these lights that is amongst the things emanating from the Light of lights is the sun. Once it gets fractionated, we see

---

[43] *Wa thiaba ..tahira,*

color. A color is more distinguishable and more individually identifiable than sunlight – it can be called 'red' or 'green' and so on – as it has a defined wave band. The more that light comes to be specific, and identifiable, the less it remains of a light. Bones and stones are also light; electrons are also light (in flashes), but they end up being a lump of stone or iron, etc. The nature of an electron is still light – modified, conditioned, changed light.

The root of everything in existence is light. That is why we say that Allah is the Light of lights (*nurul anwaar*). Every other light is varying layers of descending lights. Also, using a figure of speech we say Adam descends to this life and existence; therefore, we also say that he ascends. You have come from what is already in you, but you have to ascend to it now by choice, through struggle and striving, by turning away from the 'more changing' world to the 'less changing' world. This process continues until you find that the Light of lights never changes. Allah's original power never changes, diminishes, nor is it preoccupied by other events – that is, His attention to the ocean will not be diminished by His attention towards a leaf falling off a tree.

Final Note – Advice to the Seeker

It is vital for the Muslim seeker to know and adhere to the basic *Shar`iah* and its limitations and responsibilities. Equally it is essential to know the inner meaning of all aspects of *shar`iah's* do's and dont's. The journey begins with information and through trust and higher expectations and diligent watchfulness transformation begins to set in. Every human being is like a mirror connecting the outer world with the inner, and is evolving towards the ever-present light.

Divine light is always in the heart as a soul and the self is its companion shadow. As you grow from low to high you are moving from self to soul via the heart. You ought to maintain a healthy body, a clear mind, a pure heart and worthy companionship and you begin the practice of being prepared for the heavenly garden, whilst on the earth.

We need a set of rules to function in the world, but one general piece of advice is that whenever you feel something from the *nafs*, go against it. All the prophets, especially David, have advised that if a desire to do something overwhelms you, go against it because it will sublimate your *nafs*. If you have a choice of two possibilities, choose the one that is heavier on the *nafs*. It neutralizes you and you are no longer a slave to the desire.

One other prescription is to be honest to your state at all times; do not pretend. Express your state and be careful to mimic – not mock – higher wisdom, until it becomes real in you.

The other piece of advice is to put yourself in a symbolic grave every day – remember death.

Exercise Three – The *nafs* and the Light

***"Whenever you feel something from the* nafs, *go against it. All the prophets, especially David, have advised that if a desire to do something overwhelms you, go against it because it will sublimate your* nafs."**

What is the meaning of this statement in your own life? How do the practices of the *dīn* 'sublimate the *nafs*?

Charting the Way – Map No. 12: Exercises to Deepen Learning

(Remedies and Prescriptions for the Wayfarer)

Title:
You have come from what is already in you, but you have to ascend to it now by choice, through struggle and striving, by turning away from the 'more changing' world to the 'less changing' world.

What prescriptions and remedies does this map give to the seeker who wants to transform his/her life?

Word Length:
Between 500 and 1000 words.

Criteria:
You may use the following criteria to help you:

1. Outline briefly the factors affecting spiritual growth & the importance of will.
2. Describe the seeker's relationship with Allah.
3. Explain the seeker's attitude to his/her lower tendencies (*nafs*), virtues and vices and to change.
4. Explain the importance of spiritual practices.

You may give examples from your own or others' experience.

Charting the Way – Map No. 12: Multiple Choice Quiz
(Remedies and Prescriptions for the Wayfarer)

*The purpose of the quiz is for you to test your own understanding of this map. Choose the **BEST** answer A, B, C, or D:*

Questions:

Q 1: How can the seeker best neutralize the self's lower tendencies?
 A. By seeking spiritual growth
 B. By awareness, witnessing and avoiding the lower
 C. By having compassion for others
 D. By frequent prayer

Q 2: The child's early relationship with the mother is crucial because
 A. The child needs her love
 B. The child can't survive without the mother
 C. It lays down the basis for love and trust in God
 D. The father is less important than the mother

Q 3: Human will is a vital factor in spiritual growth because
 A. It can overcome all other shortcomings
 B. It helps a person to be independent
 C. It strengthens a person
 D. It submits to Allah's will

Q 4: It is important to remember death because
 A. We are all going to die anyway
 B. It will help us to face death more courageously
 C. It will remind us to seek security in the inner
 D. We will try to stay healthy and live longer

Q 5: We should not deny our *nafs* because
 A. We can't survive without it
 B. It is our identity
 C. We should love ourselves
 D. It is part of Allah's plan for the human being

Q 6: To get our inner in the right state we are advised to
 A. Start with the correct outer actions
 B. Practice a lot of *dhikr*
 C. Ignore our lower tendencies
 D. Spit on *Shaytan*

Answers:
1: B.
2: C.
3: A.
4: C.
5: D.
6: A.

E-Books By Zahra Publications

General E-Books on Islam

Living Islam – East and West
Shaykh Fadhlalla Haeri
Ageless and universal wisdom set against the backdrop of a changing world: application of this knowledge to one's own life is most appropriate.

The Elements of Islam
Shaykh Fadhlalla Haeri
An introduction to Islam through an overview of the universality and light of the prophetic message.

The Qur'an & Its Teachings

Journey of the Universe as Expounded in the Qur'an
Shaykh Fadhlalla Haeri
The Qur'an traces the journey of all creation, seeing the physical, biological and geological voyage of life as paralleled by the inner spiritual evolution of woman/man.

Keys to the Qur'an: Volume 1: Commentary on Surah Al-Fatiha and Surah Al-Baqarah
Shaykh Fadhlalla Haeri
The first two chapters of the Qur'an give guidance regarding inner and outer struggle. Emphasis is on understanding key Qur'anic terms.

Keys to the Qur'an: Volume 2: Commentary on Surah Ale-`Imran
Shaykh Fadhlalla Haeri
A commentary on the third chapter of the Qur'an, the family of `Imran which includes the story of Mary, mother of `Isa (Jesus).

Keys to the Qur'an: Volume 3: Commentary on Surah Yasin
Shaykh Fadhlalla Haeri
Commentary on chapter *Yasin*. This is traditionally read over the dead person: if we want to know the meaning of life, we have to learn about death.

Keys to the Qur'an: Volume 4: Commentary on Surahs Al-`Ankabut, Al-Rahman, Al-Waqi`ah and Al-Mulk
Shaykh Fadhlalla Haeri
The Shaykh uncovers inner meanings, roots and subtleties of the Qur'anic Arabic terminology in these four selected Surahs.

Keys to the Qur'an: Volume 5: Commentary on Juz' `Amma
Shaykh Fadhlalla Haeri
Insight into the last *Juz'* of Qur'an, with the objective of exploring the deeper meanings of Qur'anic Revelations.

The Essential Message of the Qur'an
Shaykh Fadhlalla Haeri
Teachings from the Qur'an such as purpose of creation, Attributes of the Creator, nature of human beings, decrees governing the laws of the universe, life and death.

The Qur'an in Islam: Its Impact & Influence on the Life of Muslims
`Allamah Sayyid M. H. Tabataba`i
`Allamah Sayyid M. H. Tabataba`i shows in this gem how the Qur'an contains the fundamental roots of Islam and the proof of prophethood as the Word of God.

The Qur'anic Prescription for Life
Shaykh Fadhlalla Haeri
Understanding the Qur'an is made accessible with easy reference to key issues concerning life and the path of Islam.

The Story of Creation in the Qur'an
Shaykh Fadhlalla Haeri
An exposition of the Qur'anic verses relating to the nature of physical phenomena, including the origins of the universe, the nature of light, matter, space and time, and the evolution of biological and sentient beings.

Sufism & Islamic Psychology and Philosophy

Beginning's End
Shaykh Fadhlalla Haeri
This is a contemporary outlook on Sufi sciences of self knowledge, exposing the challenge of our modern lifestyle that is out of balance.

Cosmology of the Self
Shaykh Fadhlalla Haeri
Islamic teachings of *Tawhīd* (Unity) with insights into the human self: understanding the inner landscape is essential foundation for progress on the path of knowledge.

Decree & Destiny (Original and a Revised Version)
Shaykh Fadhlalla Haeri
A lucid exposition of the extensive body of Islamic thought on the issue of free will and determinism.

Happiness in Life and After Death – An Islamic Sufi View
Shaykh Fadhlalla Haeri
This book offers revelations and spiritual teachings that map a basic path towards wholesome living without forgetting death: cultivating a constant awareness of one's dual nature.

Leaves from a Sufi Journal
Shaykh Fadhlalla Haeri
A unique collection of articles presenting an outstanding introduction to the areas of Sufism and original Islamic teachings.

The Chishtis: Sufi Masters of India
Muneera Haeri
In this book, Muneera Haeri recounts the lives of six early Sufis of the Chishti order. She writes for readers who are interested in Sufism, leading them to the heart of the matter via a picturesque route which traverses a landscape of ardor and devotion studded with historical facts and folk lore. This book can prove to be a feast for the trusting reader who is not blocked by cynicism in his quest for spirituality.

The Elements of Sufism
Shaykh Fadhlalla Haeri
Sufism is the heart of Islam. This introduction describes its origins, practices, historical background and its spread throughout the world.

The Garden of Meaning
Shaykh Fadhlalla Haeri
This book is about two gardens, one visible and fragrant, the other less visible but eternal. The beauty and harmony of both gardens are exposited in this magisterial volume, linking outer to inner, physics to metaphysics, self to cosmos.

The Journey of the Self
Shaykh Fadhlalla Haeri
After introducing the basic model of the self, there follows a simple yet complete outline of the self's emergence, development, sustenance, and growth toward its highest potential.

The Sufi Way to Self-Unfoldment
Shaykh Fadhlalla Haeri
Unfolding inner meanings of the Islamic ritual practices towards the intended ultimate purpose to live a fearless and honorable life, with no darkness, ignorance or abuse.

Witnessing Perfection
Shaykh Fadhlalla Haeri
Delves into the universal question of Deity and the purpose of life. Durable contentment is a result of 'perfected vision'.

Practices & Teachings of Islam

Calling Allah by His Most Beautiful Names
Shaykh Fadhlalla Haeri
Attributes or Qualities resonate from their Majestic and Beautiful Higher Realm into the heart of the active seeker, and through it back into the world.

Fasting in Islam
Shaykh Fadhlalla Haeri
This is a comprehensive guide to fasting in all its aspects, with a description of fasting in different faith traditions, its spiritual benefits, rules and regulations.

Inner Secrets of The Path
Sayyid Haydar Amuli
In this book, Seyyid Haydar Amuli – an ibn 'Arabi scholar and Gnostic from the 14th century – discusses the nature of unity, justice and prophecy as outlined by the Prophet Muhammad (peace be upon him), and how spiritual travelers should walk on the path taking to their Lord using Shari'ah. It deals specifically with the roots and branches of Islam.

Pilgrimage in Islam
Shaykh Fadhlalla Haeri
This is a specialized book on spiritual journeying, offering the sincere seeker keys to inner transformation. **Note:** It was formerly titled, *The Pilgrimage of Islam*.

Prophetic Traditions in Islam: On the Authority of the Family of the Prophet
Shaykh Fadhlalla Haeri
Offers a comprehensive selection of Islamic teachings arranged according to topics dealing with belief and worship, moral, social and spiritual values.

The Wisdom (Hikam) of Ibn 'Ata'allah: Translation and Commentary
Translation & Commentary by Shaykh Fadhlalla Haeri
These aphorisms of Ibn 'Ata'Allah, a Shadhili Shaykh, reveal the breadth and depth of an enlightened being who reflects divine unity and inner transformation through worship.

The Inner Meanings of Worship in Islam: A Personal Selection of Guidance for the Wayfarer
Shaykh Fadhlalla Haeri
Guidance for those who journey along this path, from the Qur'an, the Prophet's traditions, narrations from the *Ahl al-Bayt*, and seminal works from among the *Ahl al-Tasawwuf* of all schools of thought.

The Lantern of The Path
Imam Ja`far Al-Sadiq
Each one of the ninety-nine chapter of this book is a threshold to the next, guiding the reader through the broad spectrum of ageless wisdom, like a lantern along the path of reality.

The Sayings and Wisdom of Imam `Ali
Compiled By: Shaykh Fadhlalla Haeri
Translated By: Asadullah ad-Dhaakir Yate
Carefully translated into modern English, a selection of this great man's sayings gathered together from authentic and reliable sources.

Transformative Worship in Islam: Experiencing Perfection
Shaykh Fadhlalla Haeri with Muna H. Bilgrami
This book uniquely bridges the traditional practices and beliefs, culture and language of Islam with the transformative spiritual states described by the Sufis and Gnostics.

Talks, Interviews & Courses

Ask Course ONE: The Sufi Map of the Self
Shaykh Fadhlalla Haeri
This workbook explores the entire cosmology of the self through time, and maps the evolution of the self from before birth through life, death and beyond.

Ask Course TWO: The Prophetic Way of Life
Shaykh Fadhlalla Haeri
This workbook explores how the code of ethics that govern religious practice and the Prophetic ways are in fact transformational tools to enlightened awakening.

Friday Discourses: Volume 1
Shaykh Fadhlalla Haeri
The Shaykh addresses many topics that influence Muslims at the core of what it means to be a Muslim in today's global village.

Songs of Iman on the Roads of Pakistan
Shaykh Fadhlalla Haeri
A series of talks given on the divergence between 'faith' and 'unbelief' during a tour of the country in 1982 which becomes a reflection of the condition occurring in the rest of the world today.

The Connection Between the Absolute and the Relative
Shaykh Fadhlalla Haeri
This is a 1990 conversation with Shaykh Fadhlalla Haeri, in which he talks about wide-ranging topics on Islam and presents it as the archetypal, universal, Adamic path that began when humanity rose in consciousness to recognize duality and began its journey from the relative back to Absolute Unity.

The Spiritual Path: A Conversation with Shaykh Fadhlalla Haeri On His Life, Thought and Work
Professor Ali A. Allawi
In this wide-ranging conversation with Professor Ali Allawi, Shaykh Fadhlalla Haeri talks about his life story and the spiritual journey that he embarked on and the path he has been on ever since.

Poetry, Aphorisms & Inspirational

101 Helpful Illusions
Shaykh Fadhlalla Haeri
Everything in creation has a purpose relevant to ultimate spiritual Truth. This book highlights natural veils to be transcended by disciplined courage, wisdom and insight.

Beyond Windows
Shaykh Fadhlalla Haeri
Offering moving and profound insights of compassion and spirituality through these anthologies of connections between slave self and Eternal Lord.

Bursts of Silence
Shaykh Fadhlalla Haeri
Inspired aphorisms provide keys to doors of inner knowledge, as well as antidotes to distraction and confusion.

Essential Teachings: Bhagvan Sri Ramana Maharshi – A Sufi Interpretation of Truth Revealed
Shaykh Fadhlalla Haeri
Truth is eternal and it is not subject to certain people, place, or time. The utterances of Bhagavan Sri Ramana Maharshi carry with them the potency of what is real.

Pointers to Presence
Shaykh Fadhlalla Haeri
A collection of aphorisms providing insights into consciousness and are pointers to spiritual awakening.

Ripples of Light
Shaykh Fadhlalla Haeri
Inspired aphorisms which become remedies for hearts that seek the truth.

Sound Waves
Shaykh Fadhlalla Haeri
A collection of aphorisms that help us reflect and discover the intricate connection between self and soul.

Sublime Gems: Selected Teachings of Shaykh Abd al-Qadir al-Jilani
Shaykh Abd al-Qadir al-Jilani
Spiritual nourishment extracted from Shaykh Abd al-Qadir al-Jilani's existing works.

Autobiography

Son of Karbala
Shaykh Fadhlalla Haeri
The atmosphere of an Iraq in transition is brought to life and used as a backdrop for the Shaykh's own personal quest for self-discovery and spiritual truth.

Health Sciences and Islamic History

Health Sciences in Early Islam – Volumes 1 & 2
Collected Papers By: Sami K. Hamarneh
Edited By: Munawar A. Anees
Foreword By: Shaykh Fadhlalla Haeri
Health Sciences in Early Islam is a pioneering study of Islamic medicine that opens up new chapters of knowledge in the history of the healing sciences. This two-volume work covers the development of Islamic medicine between the 6th and 12th centuries A.D.